Not all the water in the rough rude sea
Can wash the balm off from an anointed king.
The breath of worldly men cannot depose
The deputy elected by the Lord.

William Shakespeare, *Richard II*, Act 3, scene 2

CONTENTS

PREFACE

JOSEPH SHAW

ON 8TH SEPTEMBER LAST YEAR, THE feast of the Nativity of the Blessed Virgin Mary, following the celebration of the 70th anniversary of her coronation, Queen Elizabeth II of Great Britain and Northern Ireland, and of the Commonwealth Realms,[1] died.

The coincidence of the unprecedented celebration of a monarch's 70th anniversary—her Platinum Jubilee—meant that a heightened level of national emotional and ceremonial focus on the monarchy had already begun. The death of a lady who had reigned over the United Kingdom for so long—so long, indeed, that she had become a rarity in being able to remember a time before it began—was a major moment in the life of the country. One manifestation was the queue to pay respect to her mortal remains in Westminster Hall, which at its peak was ten miles long, and took a full twenty-four hours.[2] Next to come were the extraordinarily rich symbolic displays, first of Queen Elizabeth's funeral, and then of the coronation of her son as King Charles III.

This sequence of events put Britain into an international spotlight for a prolonged period of time. The funeral and coronation were watched live by many millions of people all over the world.[3] The funeral was executed with the precision of military honours that has come to be associated with this country; the coronation with a concern for continuity and sacred symbolism that is the special mark of King Charles. Taken as a whole, the spectacle, the

---

1 Those fourteen other countries which have the British monarch as their head of state are Antigua and Barbuda, Australia, The Bahamas, Belize, Canada, Grenada, Jamaica, New Zealand, Papua New Guinea, Saint Kitts and Nevis, Saint Lucia, Saint Vincent and the Grenadines, Solomon Islands, Tuvalu.
2 According to the BBC, online report, 19 September 2022, www.bbc.co.uk/news/uk-62872323.
3 It was reported that the peak number of viewers *in the UK alone* was twenty million.

richness of symbolism, and the size of the audience, were simply staggering, and a rebuke to key tenets of modernity: individualism, a reverence for technology, and a rejection of the sacred.

Taken as a whole, the sequence of events and their execution was uniquely British. It is not just that we were fortunate to have had an extraordinarily dutiful and long-lived sovereign in Queen Elizabeth, or even that we have a popular and long-established monarchy. These factors are combined with something surprising. Our idiosyncratic political institutions, including all sorts of quaint elements, are not simply unexpected historic survivals. They have survived alongside modernity for a uniquely long time, because Britain may be said to have invented modernity. To speak only a little loosely, it was Britain that first industrialised, where the bulk of the population first moved from the country to the city, where individual liberty was first championed, where a free press first flourished. In Britain we have an ancient monarchy, certainly: the coronation ceremony dates back in substance to that of King Edgar in the year 973, as arranged by the great archbishop of Canterbury, St Dunstan, which itself derived from the imperial coronation ceremony for the Holy Roman Empire restored to the West 173 years earlier on Christmas Day 800 AD. At the same time, we have a modern monarchy, a monarchy that has seen us through the age of revolution, the age of colonialism, and the world wars; a monarchy that outfaced Hitler and outlasted Soviet Communism.

Britain's anti-modern traditions, then, have not survived by chance, as the traditions of some snow-barred alpine valley might have remained unnoticed by the passage of time. These anti-modern traditions have existed alongside modernity in its very birthplace, in conscious dialogue, conflict, and balance. Britain gave birth to modernity thanks in part to the political stability and social cohesion underpinned by her monarchy. Britain retained her ancient traditions in a conscious reaction to the atomising tendencies of the modern world, which she had experienced before any other major nation.

The tension between the old and the new in British culture gives it particular significance for the wider world. Tragically, the greatest global bastion of the anti-modern, the Catholic Church, succumbed in the twentieth century to a modern mindset in a number of ways, precipitating a crisis which will clearly take many decades to resolve. She retains the substance of her sacred office but has shed many of its symbols.

It might be suggested that, by contrast, the British monarchy retains the symbols without the substance. The symbols found in the coronation ceremony represent, for example, the Catholic doctrine that no longer animates our sovereigns in its fullness, and the executive power they no longer personally wield. However, this contrast between symbol and substance misunderstands the nature of a symbol. A symbol is a message, the assertion of a value, the expression of a view of the world. Symbols, *as symbols*, cannot lose their content, any more than a message can by definition cease to be a message. Even if the bearer of the symbol does not understand it, even if he contradicts it in some way, the symbol retains its power to speak to anyone who can perceive it. Symbols of Catholic faith point to the Catholic Faith, whether the bearer is faithful or not. Symbols of executive power point to executive power, whether the bearer exercises it personally, or delegates it. It is the Church, alas, that comes off worse in this comparison, because by rejecting her own symbols, she seems to be repudiating their message: which is her own.

As Catholic supporters of the British monarchy, the authors of the essays collected here have the task of defending the Christian symbol-complex of the monarchy which lies at the centre of British national life. Although the British monarchy retains enormous and deeply-rooted support in the country, Catholics have an advantage in understanding its meaning and its profound importance, despite the fact that nearly all of our monarchs have been in conflict with the truths of the Catholic Faith since the 1520s.

The first task of this book is to explain the place of the monarch in the British constitution, in order to address the criticisms frequently expressed by Catholics of Queen Elizabeth II's supposed failure to prevent the contradiction of natural law in the laws of her realms. This criticism must be faced, and the issues examined in some detail. As we show, it is based on a misunderstanding of the British constitution, and particularly of the phrase "Royal Assent," used when laws are passed. This does not refer to a statement by the monarch as a political actor that he or she agrees with a piece of legislation, but refers merely to the certification of the legislative process by the monarch on the advice of government ministers, advice which the monarch is obliged constitutionally to follow. The British monarch has not had a power of veto over legislation since 1688, save at the request of the very government which had sponsored the legislation (as happened in 1708),[4] or, *in extremis*, to prevent the abolition of democracy.

We are fortunate to have among the contributors to this book a Catholic constitutional lawyer, James Bogle, who is able to clarify these issues in chapters 1 and 2. Since it is also claimed that a monarch without veto cooperates wrongfully in evil if bad legislation is passed during his reign, I address this in chapter 3. Sebastian Morello addresses the real, continuing political significance of the "dignified" part of the Constitution in chapter 4.

The second part of the collection examines the coronation liturgy: as already noted, something that has evolved gradually since the time of King Edgar. Different aspects of it are examined by Sohrab Ahmari, Charles Coulombe, and Peter Day-Milne. Ahmari sets it into the context of anthropological understandings of ritual efficacy; Coulombe examines it in the context of medieval European coronation liturgies; and Day-Milne looks in more detail at Queen Elizabeth's self-understanding of her role, and at the texts and ceremonies as we experienced them in 2023.

The third and final part of this volume returns to objections to the monarchy raised by Catholics. Charles Coulombe identifies the source of much instinctive hostility to the British monarchy on the part of American Catholics as he examines the American Revolution and, in particular, the many colonists who remained loyal to the King. Bogle gives a *tour d'horizon* of the monarchy and its importance in the Anglophone world today, summarising many of the themes in the book and drawing together the threads of the argument and the reasons why Catholics have every reason

---

4   When Queen Anne was asked to withhold assent to the Scottish Militia Bill, which passed its final legislative hurdle just before political circumstances suddenly made it seem injudicious. King William III is said to have vetoed legislation on five occasions but each of these appears to have been on the advice of the government of the day. In effect, the revolution of 1688 put Parliament and the elected government above the monarch for the first time in our history.

to be grateful to be living under a monarchy, albeit a Protestant monarchy, in the twenty-first century. I examine the concept of tradition, which seems to become strangely alien even to supposedly traditional American Catholics when applied to political institutions, and Morello compares King Charles—favourably, I hasten to add—to the Emperor Nero, about whom St Peter exhorted Catholics, "honour the Emperor": "regem honorificate" (1 Pet 2:17).

In the last chapter, I set out to defend the concept of a sacred monarchy, whether this combines its sacred functions with executive powers or not. The core function of a monarch, indeed, is not leaping into an enemy town ahead of his soldiers, as did Alexander the Great (who even his own biographers thought rather excessive in that regard), but representing the rule of God to his subjects: being a link in the chain of authority, from God down to the individual. This chain implies delegation at each stage and is therefore not at all contradicted by the concept of a non-executive monarch, something that has existed at many times and places in history.

Indeed, it was before the decisive loss of executive power in 1688 that John Wilmot, Earl of Rochester, supposedly wrote on the bedchamber door of his friend, King Charles II:

> Here lies our sovereign lord the king,
> Whose word no man relies on;
> He never says a foolish thing,
> Nor ever does a wise one.

To which, perhaps apocryphally, the King replied: "'Tis most true, for my words are my own, but my actions are my ministers'."

I

THE
CONSTITUTION

The Monarchy and the British Conſtitution

JAMES BOGLE AND SEBASTIAN MORELLO

THEO HOWARD'S ARTICLE "MONARCHY and the Great Silence," published on the Catholic website called *OnePeterFive*,[1] contains assertions that we believe are serious errors, which misrepresent the true position of the British monarch, not least the late Queen Elizabeth II. Truth should be the first concern of Catholic journalists and writers, and so we wish to respond to Howard's piece in fraternal charity for the sake of the truth.

Firstly, from a practical perspective, it is our concern that Howard's article could do real harm by having the effect of encouraging secular republicanism (the only actual alternative available today) through the spreading of untruths, and serve to sour relations between nationalists and monarchists, particularly in communities where the issue is sensitive and even explosive. After all, it was not long ago that our United Kingdom was in conflict within its territories, namely in Northern Ireland, precisely over the question of whether that part of the Kingdom ought to be under the monarchy or under a republic.

The initial part of Howard's article is both typically eloquent and reasonable. Then, however, it arrives at what is described as a "quiet, regretful dissent." This "dissent," we hold, is occasioned not by any legitimate cause but due to error and misunderstanding.

That there has been a slow apostasy of the British nation away from God cannot be denied. To blame this apostasy on the late Queen, as Howard does, however, is unjust and unreasonable. Both the apostasy and moral degeneracy on display in Britain today is

---

1   23 September 2022.

equally observable across the European continent and the Americas—not least the historically very Catholic countries—so it strikes us as strange to lay this terrible trajectory at the feet of her Majesty.

More precisely, to blame the Queen for not taking an overtly partisan and political role is to fail, fundamentally, to understand the British Constitution. To call this "silence" a form of tacit consent to all the policies of successive elected governments indicates even less understanding. Accordingly, it seems a tendentious prestidigitation to claim that "Queen Elizabeth II's reign was nearly a completely unmitigated decline for the United Kingdom and the other Commonwealth Realms," as if the fact that, by convention, this period is described as her "reign," means that its decline can therefore be blamed on her personally.

Let us come, though, to the main component of Howard's "quiet, regretful dissent," which centres on a constitutional issue. We found Howard's account of the British Constitution and how it works especially misguided. Howard criticises the Queen for not vetoing the Abortion Bill of 1967. Contrary to what Howard claims, however, under the British Constitution the Royal Assent cannot be withheld by the monarch, save on the advice of ministers, or in extremely limited circumstances which, it is widely acknowledged, reduce to vetoing any bill which purports to abolish democracy.[2]

In fact, the process of Royal Assent does not even normally rest with the monarch, but with the relevant ministerial office. In the UK system, to veto a bill, a monarch would have to go out of his way to attempt to do so and, in so doing, would be attempting to usurp power that he did not possess. That, of course, would be illegal, unconstitutional, and thus a breach of both the law of the land and the Constitution, both of which the monarch swears an oath to uphold and not to breach.

Howard thus not only requires that the Queen should have breached the law and the Constitution (both of which, again, she was bound by an oath to uphold) but, in so doing, that she should have, herself, singlehandedly, destroyed democracy by overruling the settled vote of the legislative house elected by the people. Thus, Howard blames the Queen for the fact that she did not possess a certain constitutional power. We are left asking: how is that her fault?

---

2 See the next chapter for more discussion of this point.

Howard supposes that the monarch sends an "emissary" to pronounce the words of Royal Assent: *la Reyne le veult*.[3] This betrays a lack of knowledge of the actual procedure. It is the clerk of the House of Lords who pronounces these formulaic words and usually on the instruction of the Lords Commissioners who, in turn, are so instructed by the relevant minister; it is not usually on the instructions of the monarch. The words are formulaic precisely because the monarch, on his own, has no power to refuse them, save through a deliberate intervention in the rare case mentioned above. Yet Howard suggests that the monarch may simply override the UK's parliamentary democracy at will. The idea has but to be thus stated for its absurdity to be immediately self-evident. The UK is a democratic constitutional monarchy, not a monarchic dictatorship.

Such a usurpation of power, given that it would be illegal, seditious, and a very grave breach of the Constitution, would be highly immoral. One may not do evil that good may come of it, as St Paul teaches (Rom 3:8).

In the case of the Abortion Bill, the Queen acted constitutionally and could not have acted otherwise without doing evil; indeed, it is more accurate to say that she did not act at all, for she had no power to act. By claiming a right of veto that she did not constitutionally possess, she would, by that single act, have destroyed the Constitution which is the common possession of all her subjects. It is not untypical, at a period in history during which we have acquired peace-time habits, to struggle to imagine what it might be like to live in a country that is constitutionally rupturing; thus, the Queen is, in effect, being blamed for not executing a *coup d'état* that would have brought about such political chaos.

It is worth stating, lest there be any doubt, that the present authors' feelings and convictions regarding the unspeakable evil of abortion are not mild. Between us, there is over half a century of pro-life activism. But that is simply not the issue. The issue is this: did the Queen have a veto power over the bill or not? That is a matter of constitutional law. And the answer is: no, she did not have such veto power. Therefore, no one can rightly blame

---

3   "The Queen wills it." The formula, being ancient, is in Law French.

the Queen for not exercising a power she did not have. Indeed, if she had sought to exercise such a power she would have been usurping it, illegally, doing evil that good may come of it, in flat contradiction of St Paul, attempting to allow the end to justify the means—which is always immoral.

The reality, as the relevant constitutional authorities testify, is that the monarch, acting alone, has no such veto power under the British Constitution.[4]

As Howard develops his case, once again, the Queen is blamed for the declining morals of the nation by speaking of her "guilt" that "she has reigned over a period of the greatest diminishment of Christianity, and public morals, in her realm in hundreds of years, and...this will be her greatest historical legacy." Hence,

---

4 See Thomas Erskine May, *A Treatise upon the Law, Privileges, Proceedings and Usage of Parliament*, 1st ed. (1844), chs. 1 & 2; 25th ed. (2019), ch. 1; Walter Bagehot, *The English Constitution* (London: Chapman and Hall, 1867), ch. 2; A. V. Dicey, *Introduction to the Study of the Law of the Constitution* (London: MacMillan, 1885), parts I & III; V. Bogdanor, *The Monarchy and the Constitution* (Oxford: Oxford University Press, 1997); O. Hood Phillips and P. Jackson, *Constitutional and Administrative Law*, 8th ed. (London: Sweet and Maxwell, 2001), at pars. 7–10 and p. 136; A. Tomkins, *Public Law* (Oxford: Oxford University Press, 2003), at 63–64; V. Bogdanor, *The New British Constitution* (Oxford: Hart Publishing, 2009); H. Barnett, *Constitutional and Administrative Law*, 10th ed. (London: Routledge, 2013), at 325; Halsbury's *Laws of England*, vol. 20, Constitutional and Administrative Law (London: LexisNexis, 2014), at par. 18; N. Parpworth, *Constitutional and Administrative Law*, 8th ed. (Oxford: Oxford University Press, 2014), at par. 4.9; Bradley, Ewing, and Knight, *Constitutional and Administrative Law*, 16th ed. (Harlow: Pearson Education, 2015), at 19 and 207; M. Zander, *The Law-Making Process*, 7th ed. (Oxford: Hart Publishing, 2015), at 49; G. J. Wheeler, "Royal Assent in the British Constitution," *LQR* 2016, 132(Jul): 495–505. The exercise of the Royal Assent is not purely formulaic in the sense that the Crown, acting on the advice of ministers, might, in very rare circumstances (e.g., a minority government, or a colonial or devolved government), theoretically be advised to withhold assent, but such a situation is highly unlikely. What we are discussing in this article is not such a scenario but rather the Crown refusing assent *against* the advice of ministers, or *alone*. That, it is agreed by the relevant constitutional authorities, would be lawful only in the situation where the whole Constitution were about to be vitiated by, for example, extending the life of Parliament indefinitely or gerrymandering the electorate so that the government could never be ousted—that is to say, permanently destroying democracy. Otherwise, the monarch, acting alone, no more has such veto power than do any of his subjects.

6

yet again, she is blamed for a trajectory over which she had no control and which is observable across all countries gripped by the ideology of progressivist liberalism. Howard even calls this "her" legacy.

Further on, Howard claims that the monarch is not "apolitical." It is, in fact, a cardinal rule of the British Constitution that the monarch remain entirely apolitical, publicly. This does not mean that the monarch never comments about any public events whatsoever. It means that he must not interfere, in any public way, with the governmental and political process of law-making and policy-making. Thus, contrary to Howard's analogies, the non-political role of the monarch is nothing like liberal "neutrality." As a matter of provable historical fact, the Queen never breached this chief constitutional convention. To do so would, again, have been akin to an attempt to subvert democracy and the democratic process. The monarch is, and must remain, politically neutral lest he publicly interfere in the democratic process and so breach a vital constitutional convention.

Howard in fact recognises that "Monarchs cannot refuse assent, unless in an emergency, without arrogating powers that do not belong to them, and thus fundamentally damage the Constitution itself" but then proceeds to blame the Queen precisely for not doing so. Hence, she is damned if she does and damned if she does not. Howard acknowledges that such is the constitutional settlement that has obtained in Great Britain since the 1688 Revolution and yet he attempts to blame the Queen for a constitutional settlement that she inherited, and which had been in place for 300 years before her accession. No doubt Howard, like us, would prefer a constitution that afforded the monarch greater powers to rule, rather than only to reign, but that is not the Constitution we have. To hold the Queen accountable for inheriting the same flawed Constitution that we have all inherited is plainly unjust.

Howard admits that "attempting to seize or usurp power is therefore an evil" but then blames the Queen for not doing that very evil. He then asks, speculatively, "might the Queen have appealed to a higher law than the British Constitution—namely the Natural Law and Divine Positive Law on which that Constitution was originally based?" The simple answer is: she had no

7

such power. If she were to usurp power that the Constitution (of which the monarchy is merely a part) does not grant her, then, as already stated, she would have subverted and destroyed the very Constitution she pledged solemnly to defend and thus she would have sinned gravely. The locus of such a power is Parliament and chiefly the democratically elected House. It is Parliament that makes the law. If Parliament did so contrary to Natural or Divine Law—which in the case of abortion, it certainly did—then it is Parliament, not the Queen, that is guilty.

It is claimed by Howard that the Queen, when she made her Coronation Oath on 2 June 1953, somehow gained powers that the Constitution otherwise denied her. In fact, she gained no such powers. Numerous cases have been brought before the courts attempting to ascribe powers to the Queen, arising out of her Coronation Oath, powers that she simply does not have, and it is the courts who interpret and determine the limits of such powers. All such cases that have been brought before the courts have failed.

Starting in 1992, a certain Anglican clergyman, the Rev Paul Williamson, approached the courts some fourteen times to press his claim that the Coronation Oath required the Queen to veto the Priests (Ordination of Women) Measure 1993, the Bishops and Priests (Consecration and Ordination of Women) Measure 2014 and Canon No 33. The Rev Williamson continually failed so that the court, having overruled him each time, declared him a vexatious litigant forbidden to approach the court again without express permission of the court, first obtained.[5] In his case, the Court of Appeal comprehensively rejected his arguments and upheld the legality of the ordination of women in the Church of England.

The Court of Appeal held that references in the Coronation Oath to "the Protestant reformed Religion established by law," and "the settlement of the Church of England and the doctrine, worship, discipline, and government thereof, as by law established in England" referred to "such religion, church doctrine, worship, discipline, and government as so established from time to time, thereby admitting of change in accordance with the law by which

---

5   *Reverend Paul Williamson v the Archbishop of Canterbury and Others* [1996] EWCA Civ J0905-2, Court of Appeal; *R v HM Attorney General ex parte Reverend Paul Williamson* [1997] EWHC Admin 691 QB (Div Co).

it was established" (thus, ironically, admitting the very complaint that Catholicism has always had against the Church of England, namely that it is but a creature of human law). It also reminded itself that the supremacy of the Crown in Parliament (and not the Crown acting on its own) was a fundamental principle of English law, and the regularity of the consents necessary for the enactment of a statute was not justiciable in the courts (that is, not something that could be disputed through the legal system).

It is the resort of an endless succession of self-instructed and self-appointed would-be guardians of the Constitution to appeal to the Coronation Oath in an attempt to subvert the sovereignty of Parliament. Inevitably, they always end in failure. Parliament remains sovereign, not the self-appointed would-be guardians. Perhaps we may wish it were otherwise, but it is not. In short, the argument from the Coronation Oath is simply a non-argument in law.

It is a further implausibility to claim that the Queen was presented with a "dilemma" as regards Royal Assent for the abortion and same-sex marriage Acts. There was no such dilemma for the simple reason that—as noted above—the Queen had no such power of veto. One cannot be "faced with a dilemma" as to the exercise of a power that one does not possess. The present authors agree that these bills were contrary to the moral law and to the common good, but for them we cannot blame a monarch who did not propose them, pass them, or hold any power to stop them or veto them.

Then the example of King Baudouin of Belgium is raised, who abdicated for thirty-six hours in order to avoid signing a law permitting abortion.[6] Perhaps Howard imagines that all constitutions contain the same mechanisms. They do not. We are dealing with the British Constitution, not the Belgian. Belgium has a Napoleonic-style written constitution. The mechanism that exists in the Belgian Constitution, by which the government can declare the monarch temporarily unable to reign, and thereby assume the monarch's authority to enact laws, after which the government can then vote to reinstate the monarch the next day, does not exist in the UK system. Moreover, the only reason why the Belgian monarch would have had recourse to this mechanism

---

6   This took place on 4 April 1990.

in the case of an abortion bill is if he actually did possess a power of veto, and thus was faced with that apparent dilemma. The Queen, by contrast, as we have been at pains to convey, possessed no such veto power under the British Constitution. She therefore faced no such "dilemma."

The only rational argument is as follows: the Queen attracts no blame for a bill that she was powerless to veto. Accordingly, abdication would have been both unnecessary and unconstitutional. Howard fails to place the blame where it truly belongs, namely with the elected politicians who presented, pressed, and passed the legislation. Howard demonstrates a surprising naïveté when he claims that "certainly, public respect for the Queen would have made it very difficult for the government to abolish the monarchy over such a principled stand." On the contrary, such a stand would have led to the total elimination of the last remaining, and vital, *sui generis* veto power of the Crown, namely the power to veto a bill designed to abolish democracy. It is foreseeable that, in due course, when it would have been repeatedly claimed that the Crown no longer had any powers, pressure would indeed have mounted to abolish the monarchy as a whole.

Howard admits that "the Queen would have had to surrender the remaining royal prerogatives that she had," of which there is but one of any substance *sui generis* (namely, as noted, the power to veto an attempt to abolish democracy). He claims, however, that instigating a *coup d'état* by attempting to usurp a power that the Constitution does not grant the monarch, in opposition to the Abortion Bill, would have been "a sufficiently worthy cause for which to consider making such a sacrifice." In so saying, Howard fails to recognise that sacrifice must entail giving up something belonging to oneself, not something belonging to others. The Constitution belongs to all the people of the nation, not just to the monarch. It is not the Queen's personal possession for her to "sacrifice."

Howard proceeds to claim that, by such an unconstitutional action, "the consciences of the British people may have been stirred" and so there might have been "a great Christian witness." In fact, there would have likely been the very opposite—widespread dismay at the monarch attempting to usurp powers, subvert and destroy the Constitution and democracy, and a clamouring for the curtailment of the monarchical powers if not, indeed, the abolition of the monarchy as a whole. Moreover, such a "Christian witness" would have been profoundly undermined by its realisation in an act of sedition against the Constitution by the very person principally charged with upholding it.

By usurping and seizing a power which she did not have, thereby subverting and destroying the Constitution and gravely sinning, Howard argues that the Queen would have been initiating a just rebellion against a tyrannical government. In reality, she would have been staging an immoral *coup d'état* and destroying the very Constitution she swore to uphold and defend.

Moreover, rebellion is never just, as the Angelic Doctor makes clear in his work *De Regno*, chapter 7, when he writes:

> If the excess is unbearable, some have been of the opinion that it would be an act of virtue for strong men to slay the ruler and to expose themselves to the danger of death in order to set the multitude free.... But this opinion is not in accord with apostolic teaching...

In the *Summa Theologiæ* II-II, q. 42, a. 2, ad 3, to which Howard refers, St Thomas defines sedition and lays down a standard by which a ruler's government may be regarded as tyrannical: i.e., if the ruler rules for his own private good and not the common good. This, in effect, means a situation where the ruler defies and ignores the constitution and seizes power he does not legally have (i.e., the very thing that Howard expects the Queen to do). In such a case his government may legitimately be "disturbed," unless to do so would be disproportionate ("inordinate"). Thus, Howard argues against himself since, in urging the Queen to seize a power she did not have, he urges her to sedition against the Constitution and thus makes her a fit candidate for overthrow. Moreover, what this article does not say (given its brevity and focus on the definition of sedition) is who may make such a judgement and how. Howard wrongly assumes that St Thomas permits anyone to act and solely on the authority of private judgement, which would in fact render every government unsafe.

What Aquinas writes in this article must be read in the light of his other relevant writings, e.g., *De Regno*, already cited, and in the *Summa Theologiæ* II-II, q. 40, which lays down the principles of just war. The first principle is that there must be proper authority to authorise war-waging since, as St Thomas says, "it is not the business of a private individual to declare war," and in support of his position he cites St Augustine as follows: "The natural order conducive to peace among mortals demands that the power to declare and counsel war should be in the hands of those who hold the supreme authority."[7]

Moreover, one of the last works of St Thomas, his *Commentary on the Romans*, is unequivocal on this matter: no one can, by private judgement, absolve himself from allegiance to the temporal power to which he is subject unless directed to do so by a yet higher authority.[8] As St Paul writes, in a passage that St Thomas quotes in his commentary, "let everyone be subject to the governing authorities, for there is no authority except that which God has established. The authorities that exist have been established by God. Consequently, whoever rebels against the authority is rebelling against what God has instituted, and those who do so will bring judgement on themselves" (Rom 13:1–2).

Howard misunderstands the British Constitution if he supposes that the Queen, on her own, had the "supreme authority" to which Augustine refers in the aforementioned quotation. As already stated, since 1688, the sovereign power in the British Constitution is Parliament (strictly, "the Crown in Parliament") and not the monarch acting alone. Thus, the monarch may not, on his own authority, legitimately overthrow or countermand Parliament. This is the well-established constitutional principle of parliamentary sovereignty.

We agree with Howard that, by passing the Abortion Bill, the UK government did something gravely evil, worthy of public and repeated condemnation. We hold that every legitimate means ought to be embraced, constitutionally, to reverse this law.

That law, however, did not render the government illegitimate, and to seek to overthrow a legitimate government is a great evil itself. The governing part of a civil society may effectively institute certain injustices without destroying its legitimacy. And again, according to Catholic teaching, it does not belong to members of society to absolve themselves of their allegiance—unless they

---

7 St Augustine, *Contra Faustum* xxii, 75.
8 See St Thomas Aquinas, *Expositio in Romanos* xiii, lect. 1.

be absolved by a higher authority, such as a higher sovereign or higher binding international law, or, in the case of Catholic Christian states (according to the principles of Catholic political thought), by the Apostolic spiritual power of the pope.

To think otherwise is to place private interpretation above public authoritative interpretation, which is the radical Protestant error, downstream from which are all modern revolutions. Such, in fact, is to perpetuate revolution *ad infinitum.* Unless absolved of allegiance by a higher authority, one must obey the political authority in all but any compulsion to commit sin. If this were not so, St Peter and St Paul would have been committing a grave injustice by their teachings,[9] given the fact that, by such teachings, they required Christians to obey and honour Caesar, who at that time was the infamous Emperor Nero.

To accuse the Queen of sinning by refusing to veto the Abortion Bill one must first prove that she had such a power but, as a matter of law, no such power belonged to her. If the Queen possessed such a veto power over regular bills, then failure to veto immoral bills could certainly be blamed on her. But, as a matter of British constitutional law, the British monarch has no such power. We repeat once again: one cannot blame a person for failing to exercise a power that the person does not possess.

Even if we were to concede that by passing the Abortion Bill the UK government had become so tyrannical that it had lost its legitimacy—which we do not concede—nonetheless, a principle of just war doctrine is that tyranny is preferable to political collapse (e.g., Saddam Hussein is preferable to ISIS). By attempting to usurp a power that did not belong to her, and thereby rupturing the Constitution, the Queen would have potentially sent the country on the path to political collapse—a country that, as noted at the beginning of this article, faced armed conflict within its own boundaries until fairly recently.

Furthermore, by the same rules of just war, no one but the sovereign may authorise an uprising, which is a species of war. In the British Constitution, the sovereign cannot act without the advice of his ministers; and so, if the Queen had attempted to do so, she would have been acting *ultra vires* and thus her act of

---

9   See, e.g., 1 Peter 2:17; 1 Timothy 2:1–2.

"rebellion," already evil in itself, would also have been contrary to the principles of just war.

As for the notion that the Queen should be held morally responsible for the opinions of her late husband, or blamed for the conduct of her grown-up family, we deem such deliberations too frivolous to address. Such considerations distract from the constitutional errors that comprise the main thrust of Howard's case.

Regarding this central argument, Howard, towards the end of his article, attempts to sweep the rug from under the feet of those who might oppose his constitutional case on constitutional grounds. He writes that "the trouble with emphasising the virtues of the 'settled constitution' too much is that this can elide with sentimental notions about the former Queen, as well as the inherent desire for comfort and security, that we all have in this all too comfortable age."

Demeaning those who treasure a "comfortable age" strikes us as coming from one who has not experienced what it is like to be at war. One of the present authors served in Northern Ireland during the conflict in that region, and to him the "virtues of a settled constitution" and "comfort and security" are blindingly obvious.

It should be noted that, when St Paul (see 1 Tim 2:1–2) writes that "supplications, prayers, intercessions, and thanksgivings be made for all men, for kings and all who are in high positions," he does so, he tells us, precisely "that we may lead a quiet and peaceable life, godly and respectful in every way." In short, St Paul is telling us that we must be thankful for the monarch precisely because we enjoy—and should want to continue to enjoy—the "peaceable life" of a settled constitution, beyond which is only chaos.

Howard calls us to "transform all things in Christ," but he departs from the Catholic tradition by identifying such transformation with revolution. Revolutionary attempts to "transform all things in Christ" are always short-lived, for they are born from rebellion, an impulse that does not belong to the Christian but is rather the chief characteristic of the fallen angels. Instead, what lasts is the measured, lawful, constitutional transformation of nations by the Gospel, exemplified by the Middle Ages, that high moment of Christendom from which our own British Constitution comes down to us.

14

We join Howard in his lament over the present state of British society, the eroding of our organic Constitution, the gravely evil laws that have been instituted by the UK government, and above all the apostacy that we have seen sap the spiritual charity from our country. However, to blame her Majesty for this trajectory—one that is far from unique to these isles—is a serious misjudgement.

We invite our friend, Theo Howard, disagreement with whom is a very new experience for us, to retract those arguments that he has advanced which blame her Majesty for that over which she had no power, and thus bears no guilt.

2

Queen Elizabeth II
and the Royal Assent

JAMES BOGLE

I T HAS BEEN REPEATEDLY ARGUED, NOT
least in American media and journals, that the late Queen
Elizabeth II of Great Britain and Northern Ireland, whilst
exemplary in every way in her personal life, was nevertheless
responsible for permitting very seriously immoral legislation to
pass the UK Parliament during her time as Queen.

This argument is not only wrong, it is very ill-informed. The
Queen had no blame for such legislation since she had no power
whatsoever to stop it. The blame lies solely with the elected politicians who introduced and passed the legislation. Unlike the US
President, the British monarch, being unelected, has no power of
veto over bills passed by the Houses of Parliament. The so-called
"Royal Assent" is no free assent. It is a largely ceremonial process
which represents no more than a formal certification that a bill has
passed the Houses of Parliament and may now be declared law.

Moreover, this so-called "Royal Prerogative" (with some very
rare and arcane exceptions) cannot be exercised save on the
"advice" of the UK Prime Minister or relevant minister and that
"advice" must be followed. Ministerial "advice" to the monarch is,
in effect, an ineluctable demand by the government of the day,
on behalf of the popularly elected House, which the monarch
is obliged to obey and follow. The monarch is thus obliged by
the Constitution to give that certification once advised by the
relevant minister that a bill has passed its stages and that he
must certify. This has been our constitution since the Revolution
of 1688 which effectively put Parliament above the Crown. It is
now our constitution, like it or not.

Moreover, the Constitution being morally neutral, it must be obeyed, not least by the monarch who sits at its apex and has sworn to uphold it. If the Queen had disobeyed the Constitution, she would have been committing a gravely evil act and, in effect, seizing a power that she did not have. That would be an unconstitutional *coup d'état* which would be a form of sedition. She would have been claiming the right to override the democratically elected Parliament, elected by the people. The Constitution forbids this and has done so since 1688. Our present system of government has been described by some scholars as a "crowned democracy" which is largely accurate. We do not much differ from other countries, including republics, in that respect. The only difference is that our largely honorary head of state is unelected.

There is an exception to the rule that the British monarch has no discretion to interfere in the legislative process. It is generally agreed by the relevant constitutional authorities that the British monarch may, on his own authority, veto a bill extending the life of Parliament indefinitely or gerrymandering the electorate so that the government could never be ousted—that is to say, a bill seeking to destroy or abolish democracy. For similar reasons, the monarch also has power, acting alone on his own discretion, to dismiss a prime minister who refuses to resign after losing the confidence of the House of Commons, the popularly elected House. These exceptions are absolutely vital and make the monarch's position as important today as ever it was. They provide the immediate and decisive answer to those who rather tritely ask "well, what is the point of the monarch, then?" One might just as well ask the same question about the presidents of most republics, since many of them do not even have the power to veto a bill that would abolish democracy.

That exceptional power is a vitally important final protection for democracy and preventative against tyranny. For the lack of such a monarch with such a power, Germany in 1933 fell under the power of the Nazis. If Germany had then still been a monarchy, even if the monarch had as limited powers as the British monarch, the King could have vetoed the bills abolishing democracy and required Hitler to submit to an election. The result would undoubtedly have been the fall of the Nazis, the prevention of the Second World War, and the saving of a hundred million lost lives.

This preventative power is, then, a vitally important final power which the monarch retains. Nor is it a merely chimerical power since it has been activated in other common law countries such as Australia when, in 1975, the Queen's official representative, the Governor General, Sir John Kerr, after months of the Labour prime minister trying to govern without supply (i.e., money) refused him by the Senate, dismissed the Prime Minister, dissolved both Houses of Parliament and required a new caretaker prime minister to call a General Election. The Labour Party then lost the General Election and the Opposition Liberal Party won with the biggest ever majority in Australian political history, a clear democratic endorsement of the Governor General's vice-regal act.

Now, Australia has a written constitution, so those vice-regal powers are set out in black and white and are more extensive than those of the British monarch; nevertheless, the principle was re-established and preserved. The head of state must protect the Constitution and the people from tyranny, if it becomes necessary.

Otherwise, the British monarch, acting alone, has no more veto power over legislation than do any of his subjects. And it has been that way for a very long time. Here is what renowned and oft-quoted Victorian constitutional expert, Walter Bagehot, wrote in his famous work *The English Constitution* in 1867:

> The popular theory of the English Constitution involves two errors as to the Sovereign. First, in its oldest form at least, it considers him as an "Estate of the Realm," a separate coordinate authority with the House of Lords and the House of Commons. This and much else the Sovereign once was, but this he is no longer. That authority could only be exercised by a monarch with a legislative veto. He should be able to reject bills, if not as the House of Commons rejects them, at least as the House of Peers rejects them. But the Queen has no such veto. She must sign her own death warrant if the two Houses unanimously send it up to her. It is a fiction of the past to ascribe to her legislative power. She has long ceased to have any.[1]

Even when Queen Anne, in 1708, refused assent to the Scottish Militia Bill, the last time ever that such a refusal was attempted,

---

1 Walter Bagehot, *The English Constitution* (Eastbourne: Sussex Academic Press, 1997), 33.

it was done entirely on the advice of her ministers. It was not a unilateral act by the Crown, as some have falsely imagined. The Scottish Militia Bill 1708 had been passed by the House of Commons and House of Lords, of the newly conjoined Parliament of Great Britain,[2] in early 1708. The bill's long title was "An Act for settling the Militia of that Part of Great Britain called Scotland." Its object was to arm the Scottish militia, which had not been re-created at the Restoration. The bill was meant to be part of the parliamentary unification of Scotland and England under the Acts of Union 1707. On the day the bill was meant to be signed, news came that the French were sailing toward Scotland for the planned invasion of 1708 and there was suspicion that a Scottish militia might side with the French. Ministers could have taken steps in Parliament to secure a repeal of the bill but that would have taken too long, and so they opted for a simple veto. In the light of the news, support for a veto was strong. Thus, on 11 March 1708, Queen Anne withheld Royal Assent on the advice of her ministers, for fear that the proposed Scottish militia might become hostile to the government. Note that, even then, the monarch had no independent discretion to veto a bill. Then, as now, she was obliged to follow the "advice" of her ministers which, as stated, above, is, in effect, a demand of the government of the day, on behalf of the popularly elected House, which the monarch is obliged to obey and follow.

The last time the idea of refusing Royal Assent was seriously discussed was with King George V as regards the Irish Home Rule Bill of 1913–14, the first such bill to have been presented for Royal Assent under the new Parliament Act 1911 (that is, without the consent of the Lords). Constitutional expert Professor Vernon Bogdanor describes the events surrounding this crisis in his 1995 book *The Monarchy and the Constitution*. Pressure for the veto came not from the government but from the Conservative Opposition.

The claim that the Royal Prerogative still included the power to refuse Royal Assent, if so advised by ministers, made a reappearance in 2019 with the proposed Cooper-Letwin and Benn-Burt Bills designed to resolve the deadlock caused by the Fixed Term Parliaments Act 2011 which prevented the government calling an election to resolve its minority position and potentially allowed Parliament

---

2   That is, shortly after the Acts of Union of 1707 united the Scottish and English parliaments.

to reverse "Brexit" (the decision for Britain to exit the European Union). It was claimed by some that, if legislation would otherwise be passed by an abuse of constitutional process and principle facilitated by a rogue Speaker, the government could legitimately advise the monarch to refuse assent and so veto the bill.[3]

A huge furore was caused and many dissenting voices weighed in. Professors Jeff King and Mark Elliott argued that there was no existing mechanism through which the refusal of assent could be effected, and that assent was not an action which relied on the advice of ministers but depended solely on the fact that Parliament had passed a bill.[4]

Professor John Finnis, partly disagreeing with Professor Mark Elliott, in an article in the *Daily Telegraph* published on 1 April 2019 ("Only one option remains with Brexit—prorogue Parliament and allow us out of the EU with no deal"), and in a subsequent blog ("Royal Assent—A Reply to Mark Elliott," UK Constitutional Law Association blog, 8 April 2019) argued—correctly, in my view—that the Lord Chancellor could delay seeking the Royal Assent (rather than the Prime Minister advising against granting it), possibly up to and beyond the point of a prorogation.

However, all sides were in agreement that the prerogative power to withhold assent could only conceivably be invoked at a moment of profound constitutional crisis[5]—for example, where a prime minister sought to abolish democracy. Australian professor of Law, Anne Twomey, in chapter 9 of her book *The Veiled Sceptre: Reserve Powers of the Heads of State in Westminster Systems,* largely concurred.[6]

---

3 See Stephen Laws and Richard Ekins, *Endangering Constitutional Government: The Risks of the House of Commons Taking Control* (London: Policy Exchange, 2019), 3.

4 Jeff King, "Can Royal Assent to a Bill Be Withheld If So Advised by Ministers?," UK Constitutional Law Association blog, 5 April 2019; and Mark Elliott et al. "Royal Assent: Letter to *The Times,*" Public Law for Everyone blog, 3 April 2019. The latter letter attracted many very prominent names in the law, both academic and professional, including Lord Pannick KC and Dinah Rose KC.

5 See, for example, Robert Craig, "Could the Government Advise the Queen to Refuse Royal Assent to a Backbench Bill?," UK Constitutional Law Association blog, 22 January 2019; G. J. Wheeler, "Royal Assent in the British Constitution," *LQR* 2016, 132(Jul): 495–505.

6 Anne Twomey, *The Veiled Sceptre: Reserve Powers of the Heads of State in Westminster Systems* (Cambridge: Cambridge University Press, 2018), 646–47.

Neither the then Prime Minister, Rt Hon Theresa May MP, nor her successor, Rt Hon Boris Johnson MP, heeded any of the suggestions that they might advise the Queen to exercise a royal veto, either on supposed grounds of unconstitutionality or simply because they disagreed with legislation passed by Parliament. The Leader of the House, Sir Jacob Rees-Mogg MP, in response to a question about whether the government would seek to deny the bill Royal Assent, said: "The law will be followed. We are a country that follows the rule of law and this government assiduously follows constitutional conventions." It seems therefore that even refusal of assent on the advice of a minister is not constitutionally possible, though some scholars and lawyers might still disagree.

Later, as is well known, Mr Johnson's advice to the monarch to prorogue Parliament, which was duly followed, was, in due course, impugned by the UK Supreme Court in the *Miller II* case.[7] According to Professor John Finnis in his article entitled "The unconstitutionality of the Supreme Court's prorogation judgment,"[8] it was an unprecedented challenge, in effect, to a royal prerogative power that is, and always has been, non-justiciable (i.e., cannot be contested in the courts), and, indeed, Baroness Hale, in a Channel Islands case five years earlier, had ruled so in a judgment.[9] Some will remember that she was the presiding

---

7 *R (Miller) v the Prime Minister and Cherry v Advocate General for Scotland* [2019] UKSC 41.

8 John Finnis, "The unconstitutionality of the UK Supreme Court's prorogation judgment," Policy Exchange, London, 28 September 2019, later published in (of all places) *The UK Supreme Court Year Book.*

9 Ibid., p. 8, par. 5. Professor Finnis writes: "And the Supreme Court owed us all an answer to the argument put to it in the final submissions of counsel for the Prime Minister and the Advocate General":

> In *R (Barclay) v Lord Chancellor* [2014] UKSC 54 . . . the Supreme Court unanimously held that the granting of Royal Assent was a proceeding in Parliament. That is significant because Royal Assent may be granted by Commission, including by the same commission which provides for the prorogation of Parliament. Per Baroness Hale of Richmond at §48: "Nor is the analogy [of assent to Laws passed by the Chief Pleas of the Island of Sark] with Royal Assent to Acts of the United Kingdom Parliament exact: the Queen in Parliament is sovereign, and its procedures cannot be questioned in the courts of the United Kingdom."
>
> So, in 2014, in the Supreme Court, actions of the Crown that directly concern proceedings in and of Parliament are procedures

judge of the UK Supreme Court who was seen wearing a spider brooch and was labelled by the media "the Spider lady."

Over and above all these fascinating debates, what, however, is crystal clear, and all sources agree without any dissent, is that no monarch, since 1688, may, on his or her own initiative, veto any bill with the exception of a bill to abolish democracy.

It is no different in most modern republics. President Mitterrand once described the role of the French President in promulgating laws under the French constitution as, in effect, no more than that of a magnified "notary."[10]

In fact, the so-called "Royal Assent" is no form of assent at all. It entails no discretionary act by a monarch who is simply bound to follow the "advice" of the relevant minister. In effect, therefore, all that the monarch does in exercising the Royal Assent is to certify that, on the advice of the relevant minister, a bill has passed all its parliamentary stages. What has made the contents of the bill law is not so much Royal Assent but the votes in Parliament and the workings of the Constitution. The monarch is doing no more than acknowledging what is already a fact, that is, that Parliament wills a bill to become law. The monarch has no power whatsoever to delay or challenge that bill, let alone to veto it, once the relevant minister has advised the monarch to certify its passage by the so-called "Royal Assent."

Indeed, the very mechanism of Royal Assent is done in the relevant minister's office or, at most, by three Lords Commissioners, appointed by the Prime Minister, sitting in the House of Lords, who command the clerk of the House to signify assent in the customary law French—"*le Roy le veult*," "the King wishes it." In fact, the King's wishes have nothing whatever to do with it. It is entirely the wish of the Parliament, the ministers, and the operation of the Constitution.

---

of Parliament itself (not merely of the Crown)—procedures that, echoing the Bill of Rights, "cannot be questioned in the courts." But [perversely, and according to the Supreme Court] in 2019 they "cannot sensibly be described" as proceedings in Parliament, and can be questioned, impeached for some flaw in their antecedents, and judicially declared to be nullities even when they do take place in—within—Parliament.

10 "L'entretien télévisé du président de la République," *Le Monde*, 16 July 1993.

Many people are misled by the term "Royal Assent" into thinking that there is an element of royal discretion. In reality, there is none whatsoever. The monarch does no more than simply acknowledge a process. The exception is a bill to abolish democracy. Thus, if a monarch were to attempt to usurp a veto power that he does not possess this would simply be a *coup d'état* and an outright sedition against the Constitution and—worse—by the very person who is most charged with upholding the Constitution.

Sedition is not only a crime; it is morally evil. For example, the foremost Roman Catholic theologian, St Thomas Aquinas, taught that sedition is a grave evil.[11] So does the Catechism of the Roman Catholic Church.[12] It would still be evil even if it were done to try to achieve a good, even a very great good: one may not do evil that good may come of it, in the words of St Paul.[13]

For these reasons, the Queen was bound to obey the Constitution, to keep silent and not to comment publicly lest she be seizing a power she did not have and thereby be doing a grave evil. Indeed, even for the monarch to voice any public dissent would be a breach of the Constitution as it would be tantamount to intermeddling with the supremacy of Parliament and of the democratically elected House.

Abdication would similarly be a breach of the Constitution and, indeed, an even more serious breach since it would occasion a constitutional crisis, causing a rupture of the Constitution every much as bad as a purported refusal to certify a bill, and would thus be equally unlawful and morally repugnant. Since mere certification that a bill has passed its parliamentary stages could not ever found a basis for abdication and the creation of a constitutional crisis and rupture, even to attempt abdication would be seriously wrong morally.

Therefore, critics of the Queen have simply misunderstood her role and her powers. They ascribed to her power over legislation which she simply did not have. The cause and responsibility lie with the elected politicians, whom the monarch did not elect, and with the Constitution, which the monarch did not devise but inherited, like her forebears, from 1688.

---

11   St Thomas Aquinas, *Summa Theologiæ*, II-II, q. 42, aa. 1 & 2 (citing 2 Cor 12:20).
12   See nos. 2238–40 of the *Catechism of the Catholic Church*.
13   Romans 3:8.

Provided human positive law does not defy divine or natural law, then it must be obeyed. This is common morality and, moreover, what the Roman Catholic Church's doctrine[14] teaches. The British Constitution does not enjoin intrinsic evil and must therefore be obeyed, not least, as I said above, by the monarch who sits at its apex. The Constitution, in requiring the monarch, when advised by a minister, to certify that a bill has passed its parliamentary stages, is not requiring the monarch to do anything intrinsically evil. Merely to certify that a bill has passed both Houses of Parliament is not intrinsically evil. Therefore, a human positive law that requires the monarch to do so must be obeyed and to disobey it would be evil, even if it were disobeyed with the aim of achieving a good thereby.

Moreover, this applies whether the monarch is an Anglican, a Methodist, a Presbyterian, a Jew, a Muslim, a Buddhist, or a daily communicant Catholic.

I might add that the British monarch, in this respect, is in no different position from that of the presidents of most European republics. For example, Article 13.3 of the Irish constitution states:

> 1° Every bill passed or deemed to have been passed by both Houses of the *Oireachtas* [the Irish Parliament, *Seanad* and *Dail*] shall require the signature of the President for its enactment into law.
>
> 2° The President shall promulgate every law made by the Oireachtas.

The Irish President, like the British monarch, therefore, has no power to veto a bill, no matter how evil or immoral it may be. The most he can do, under Article 26, is to refer it, within 7 days, to the Irish Supreme Court for a decision as to its constitutionality, though not as to its morality.

Similar provisions apply to the presidents of France, Germany, Austria, Poland, Hungary, Czechia, and many others (but not the US or, apparently, Italian presidents who do have an actual veto).

Yet the critics of the Queen do not apply the same standard of criticism to these presidents. A not untypical example of this kind of ill-instructed criticism of the late Queen is seen in an article, published 30 November 2022, on the *Voice of the Family*

---

14 See nos. 1898–1900 of the *Catechism of the Catholic Church*.

website[15] by British-born academic, Dr Alan Fimister, of the *Dialogos* Institute. Uncharacteristically, Fimister has not thought through his case well and as a result makes a string of fundamental errors. However, these errors are not untypical of much ill-informed criticism of the late Queen.

He first launches into an attack on the Anglican Church as if that were sufficient to ground his thesis that the late Queen was responsible for all the immoral legislation passed during her years as Queen. As I say above, the fact that the Queen was an Anglican is absolutely irrelevant and redundant as regards the question of her involvement in the legislative process in the UK. Her role is the same constitutionally regardless of religious affiliation.

The idea of a marriage of Church and State is a profoundly Catholic idea, being neither secularist, like most modern republics, nor theocratic, like many Islamic states, but a dyarchy as taught by Pope St Gelasius I in his famous letter to the Emperor Anastasius entitled *Famuli Vestræ Pietatis*, the original blueprint for Catholic Christendom. This dyarchical idea was abandoned by many of the Protestant rebel states but not, by any means, all. Thus, in England, King Henry VIII retained a form of dyarchical government but one that repudiated the authority of the Holy See.

Nevertheless, this dyarchical marriage of Church and State is still the basis of our British Constitution and part of what makes us, at least nominally, a Christian constitutional monarchy, with the State Church being Anglican. Ireland, by contrast, is an entirely secularist state expressly treating all religions and none as equal, whether Christian, Muslim, Buddhist, Hindu, Humanist, or whatever. In stark contrast to Christian (albeit Protestant) Britain, Ireland is now a militantly secular state. That the Irish live under a fully secular neo-heathen state, and have done since 1922, was made clear by Mr Justice Barrington when, giving the lead judgement of the Irish Supreme Court in *Corway v Independent Newspapers Ltd*,[16] he said, point blank, at paragraph 26 of the judgment: "the 1922 constitution was a totally secular constitution."

The Irish Supreme Court also added that the few additions to the Irish constitution, made in 1937 by Eamon de Valera,

---

15 "Absolutely null and utterly void," *Voice of the Family Digest*, no. 81, 30 November 2022, https://voiceofthefamily.com/absolutely-null-and-utterly-void/.
16 [1999] IESC 5.

detracted but little from the Irish constitution's secularity and, in any case, these were removed by the Fifth Amendment in 1972. It is thus a simple fact that Ireland's Constitution is entirely secular in contrast to the British Constitution which remains a Christian Constitution, albeit the State Church is Anglican. Critics of the late Queen completely overlook these facts.

Fimister writes further, erroneously, that:

> The sovereign of the United Kingdom can claim that "convention"—that is ... customary public law—requires that he withhold assent to bills passed by both Houses of Parliament only upon the advice of his ministers. Customary public law cannot exculpate him from enacting *per se* immoral "laws" any more than a soldier can excuse a war crime on the grounds that he was "only obeying orders."

This is not only erroneous; it is also irrational. The British monarch makes no such "claim" since the British monarch has no such power of assent, as already stated above. Fimister simply fails to understand the nature of the British Constitution, possibly because he is not a lawyer but an historian. The British monarch needs no "exculpating" since he has no power to "enact," and so cannot "enact," any laws, whether *per se* immoral or moral. Accordingly, the military analogy fails, since a soldier executing a war crime certainly *does* have power to execute it.

Many critics of the monarch, despite not being constitutional lawyers, nevertheless claim to know better than the principal constitutional authorities as to what British constitutional law stipulates. The constitutional authorities all concur that the monarch has no power to veto or delay legislation passed by the Houses of Parliament and that the term "Royal Assent" is a legal fiction. Thus, the monarch's personal assent is not involved at all, save for the abolition of democracy exception. But even the abolition of democracy exception would require the monarch to consult the leaders of the Opposition before taking any action and, in effect, to respond to their advice in a similar manner as he would normally respond to the advice of government ministers. In protecting democracy, the monarch would have to consult democratically, as one might expect. The difference is that he would then be consulting the Opposition rather than the government.

Undeterred, however, Fimister declares, on his own entirely unsupported, solipsistic authority, that our constitutional system is "immoral." Yet, as already explained, it is almost exactly the same system, as regards assent by a head of state, as obtains in most European republics. Where is the denunciation of those systems as "immoral"? One may look but one will not find it.

Fimister's basis for claiming the "system is immoral" is also faulty and erroneous. This is the curious basis upon which he alleges such "immorality":

> Pope Zachary advised Pepin the Short that it is not appropriate for someone to bear the name of king while exercising no actual power. By such an arrangement, a person is made morally responsible for actions over which he has little real power.

Prescinding from the fact that such a purely political claim by Pope St Zachary could not have been a doctrinal statement, that is not, in fact, what this pope said. Pope St Zachary, then ruling the Duchy of Rome, was imperilled by the Lombards and so sought to make a political alliance with Pepin the Short, later King of the Franks, in the hope and expectation that Pepin would come to his aid against the Lombards, which, in due course, he did.

Answering a strategically and politically motivated question from Pepin, then the Frankish Mayor of the Palace who planned to take the throne from the weak Merovingian King Childeric III, Zachary rendered the virtually inevitable opinion that it was better that Pepin should be king given that Childeric had lost virtually all power. Shortly thereafter, the Frankish nobles decided to abandon Childeric in favour of Pepin. They had that constitutional power and right under the Frankish system. Pope Zachary was not making a generic, doctrinal statement about all royal power but a very time-specific, politically motivated comment as part of a temporary, contingent political policy. This was, as much as anything, a political ploy on the part of Pope St Zachary to back the Frankish strong man who would, in turn, defend the Papal Duchy of Rome from attack by the Lombards.

This is nowhere near Fimister's claim that Pope St Zachary, in some kind of universal doctrinal sense, was opposed to the modern constitutional idea of strict restrictions on the powers of an unelected monarch. The analogy therefore fails.

Neither did Pope St Zachary say that such restrictions made "a person morally responsible for actions over which he has little real power" nor, indeed, anything like it. The less real power a moral actor has, the less moral responsibility he has. So much is morally and philosophically obvious. In the case of the British monarch, he has no power at all to veto or delay legislation and thus has no moral responsibility for the same. One cannot be morally blamed for failing to exercise a power one does not have.

Fimister further misses the point again in the only paragraph in his whole article that comes close to addressing the argument at issue, when he writes:

> Even if we were to imagine *what is clearly not the case*— that the assent given by the monarch is universally recognised as *purely ceremonial,* such that he is not morally compromised in any way by the assertion that the bill under consideration reflects his will—this would still achieve nothing, because such a false assertion *would itself be gravely immoral*... It remains the case that the fact of the monarch's assent is being solemnly asserted in parliament by commissioners *purportedly working for him* and this assertion is a necessary precondition of the bill becoming law. He is *still able to instruct his ministers not to permit this ceremony to occur, or even to repudiate it by a public statement.*[17]

Not only is this wrong, as a matter of law and constitutional convention, but it betrays a failure to understand the British Constitution and what the constitutional authorities actually say.[18] Those authorities simply say that the "Royal Assent" is an obligatory formality and is not the monarch's will—period.

As mentioned elsewhere, the position of the monarch is no different from that of most republican presidents when it comes to the issue of assenting to legislation, but you will find no parallel criticism of them by Fimister. His is a purely one-sided criticism evidencing a *parti prise* against the monarch and a bias and prejudice that taints his whole argument.

It is also an error to claim that the Lords Commissioners "work" for the monarch. They do not. They work for Parliament and, in

---

17   Emphasis added.
18   See references given in note 3 on page 6.

the British Constitution since 1688, Parliament, not the King, is sovereign. To blame the Queen for this is thus to blame her for a constitution that became law nearly 300 years before she was even born, which is plainly an untenable criticism.

It is also an error to claim that the monarch "is still able to instruct his ministers not to permit this ceremony to occur, or even to repudiate it by a public statement." In fact, the reverse is true. The monarch has no power to instruct ministers. On the contrary, it is the elected ministers who, in effect, "instruct" the monarch when they "advise" him. The criticisms are thus wholly misconceived.

Indeed, in a letter to *The Times* newspaper at the time of the Brexit crisis in 2019, a large number of law professors, and some of the most prominent Queen's Counsel (senior trial lawyers) of the day, reaffirmed the accepted view that "Royal Assent" is a pure formality. Indeed, they agreed that it could not even be withheld on the "advice" (for which read "orders") of the Prime Minister, once a bill had passed the Houses of Parliament. They argued that the monarch could not be "advised" by ministers to refuse to certify what was already a *fait accompli*, namely that a bill had passed its parliamentary stages.

Fimister claims that "of course, no one is suggesting any pro-life...coups" but that, in fact, is precisely what he is arguing for—a royal *coup d'état*.

Finally, he cites the example of Eleazar, one of the chief scribes in Israel, in the second chapter of the Book of Maccabees, who refused, when ordered, to eat swine's flesh, or even to pretend to do so because it would savour of dissembling. The analogy again fails because Eleazar had the power to choose to eat, or not to eat. The British monarch has no power to veto or to delay a bill and thus has no need to pretend either way. Moreover, to certify that a bill has passed its parliamentary stages is not an intrinsically evil act, whereas Eleazar believed that eating swine's flesh was.

Fimister also quotes St John Henry Newman, inappositely and out of context. Newman was a known political conservative who was an admirer of Queen Victoria. In this respect, Newman never once denounced the Queen for failing to seize a veto power she did not have against immoral legislation (such as, for example, the Matrimonial Causes Act 1857 introducing civil divorce). Newman, having a better understanding of the British Constitution, and of the doctrine of parliamentary sovereignty, knew that the Queen did not have power to stop these bills, however immoral. Fimister, alas, does not seem to know this.

Others have argued that the monarch is morally responsible for immoral laws passed by Parliament by virtue of being the efficient cause of a bill becoming law since her assent makes the bill law. This, too, is constitutionally and morally misconceived. She is no more the morally responsible efficient cause of a bill becoming law, and perhaps even less so, than is the doorkeeper of the House of Commons the morally responsible efficient cause of the bill becoming law because he opened the doors of the House to MPs or failed to lock them in until they reversed the immoral bill in question.

St Thomas teaches[19] that some acts can be indifferent morally, like stroking one's beard or moving a hand or foot, but that all acts of a moral agent proceeding from deliberative reason are either moral or immoral. However, if the act is too remote from the end, or the end is not foreseeable, then the act is not culpable and the moral agent is not guilty of any evil.

Certifying, on the advice of a minister, that a bill has passed its parliamentary stages is not an intrinsically evil act. Indeed, it not even a link in the causative chain since it merely acknowledges and confirms what is already a *fait accompli*, that is, that the bill has passed its parliamentary stages. Few now pretend that a refusal to certify would somehow defeat the will of Parliament.[20] Conversely, a refusal to certify, being a rupture of the Constitution, a revolutionary sedition and a *coup d'état*, would be a very serious evil and one directly and efficiently caused by the monarch himself, Charles Mountbatten-Windsor, on his own initiative. It therefore would be a very grave evil and so may not be done.

---

19 *Summa Theologiæ*, I-II, q. 18, a. 9, "Whether an individual action can be indifferent."
20 Remarkably, once the Supreme Court in *Miller II* had ruled that the 2019 prorogation was illegal, both the Speaker of the Commons and the Lord Speaker of the Lords ruled—wrongly—that this must mean that the bill that had been given Royal Assent that day must also fall and so must be advanced again for Royal Assent. This was entirely fallacious since the Supreme Court itself acknowledges that the giving of Royal Assent is non-justiciable and they could not impugn it. Such was the constitutional confusion created by the UK Supreme Court's judgment in *Miller II*.

The reality is that the late Queen Elizabeth II was a model of virtue, selfless duty, and obedience to the law and the Constitution, as well as a devout and prayerful Christian believer, albeit a Protestant one. In her very public witness to her belief in Christ, and her love of Him, she was virtually unique among world leaders. It takes a peculiar degree of perversity for any Christian subject of that late Queen to go out of his way to attack her, particularly when the substance of the attack is upon a set of rules and norms which are largely no different from those that apply to the presidents of most republics, none of whom is subject to criticism by the critics of the Queen in anything like the vituperative and unjust manner in which they criticise her late Majesty. The critics simply measure with double standards.

Indeed, those who attack the Queen and the monarchy, fail, in their haste, to recognise that the only alternative to Christian monarchy (albeit a Protestant monarchy) is neo-heathen, secularist republicanism of the sort that is increasing all across the face of the globe. There is no other present alternative. Thus, in attacking the Queen and monarchy, the critics are doing no more than throwing fuel onto the flames of that same neo-heathen, secularist republicanism which the enemies of Christianity wish to see imposed across the whole globe. They are also, in effect, championing a very serious rupture of the Constitution by a royal *coup d'état* which could have the most far-reaching and damaging consequences, not excluding revolution.

That any Catholic should wish such a fate upon his own nation is surely the last word in perversity. Yet, those who unjustly attack our late Queen and monarchy are risking just that. One can but hope that they wake up and see reason sooner rather than later.

3
The Monarchy and Responsibility for Legislation

JAMES BOGLE

D R ALAN FIMISTER'S ARTICLE "TO GOD alone be the honour and the glory,"[1] published on the website of the British-based lay Catholic initiative *Voice of the Family*, is clearly written with good intentions. However, it misrepresents the true position of the British monarch, not least the late Queen Elizabeth II, and that on a very serious and important issue.

Unfairly disparaging the monarch effectively encourages secular republicanism, which is the only alternative available today and, moreover, can undermine relations between nationalist and monarchist, not least in sensitive communities like those in Northern Ireland where conflict has raged on that issue for many decades. Moreover, it is in just that very Province that key moral issues such as abortion and the role of the family have been most hotly contested, with the government in Westminster imposing legislation upon the Province, by ministerial *fiat* and against the will of the majority of the people living there. The blame for this lies with the ministers and Parliament and not with the monarch who has no power to prevent it.

I start, however, with the title of his article.

In adopting the old Scriptural motto, *soli Deo gloria*, Fimister mistranslates the Latin in the very same way that the radical Protestant rebels of the sixteenth century did: "to God alone."

---

1 Published at *Voice of the Family Digest* No. 74 of 12 October 2022, https://voiceofthefamily.com/to-god-alone-be-the-honour-and-the-glory/.

Indeed, that mistranslation became one of the 5 *solæ* summarising the fundamental beliefs of those same radical Protestant rebels: (1) grace alone, (2) faith alone, (3) Christ alone, (4) Scripture alone, and (5) God alone—*soli Deo gloria*. All these *solæ* were understood in a heretical sense and so were condemned by the Magisterium of the Roman Catholic Church.

The true sense of *soli Deo*—"to the one only God"—is seen in its biblical context. In the Vulgate Latin approved by the Catholic Church, 1 Timothy 1:17 reads thus: "Regi autem sæculorum immortali invisibili *soli Deo* honor et gloria in sæcula sæculorum amen," meaning "Now to the king of ages, immortal, invisible, *the one only God*, be honour and glory for ever and ever. Amen." The difference in meaning is striking and vital because the radical Protestant rebels meant by the phrase that only God should be given honour and glory, not the Virgin Mary, not the saints, not popes, bishops, magistrates, kings, or emperors. Ironically, however, these same radical Protestant rebels (or at least most of them) nevertheless continued to believe in the doctrine of the Immaculate Conception of the Blessed Virgin Mary, which is a Catholic doctrine meaning that the Virgin Mary was conceived free of any taint of Original Sin and should be given appropriate honour and glory for the same.

It was central to radical Protestant teaching that, as Luther taught, the baptised are not cleansed of their sin but are, instead, not much more than "dung heaps covered in snow," all equally evil, and God, with His grace (the "snow"), merely cloaks their evil (the "dung") as if to hide it. Thus, by the lights of such radical Protestantism, St Francis is as evil as Stalin and St Teresa of Avila as evil as Pol Pot but Christ, through His crucifixion and grace, simply "hides" all their evil.[2] Far from being "dung hills covered in snow," man grows in glory as he accepts redemption and grace (not least through the sacraments) and the more he does so, the more glorious he becomes.

---

2 As Luther put it: *Pecca fortiter, sed crede fortius*—"sin strongly, but believe more strongly still"—for it is the original Lutheran Protestant belief that the elect go to heaven merely by believing in Christ, no matter how much they may sin in their daily lives. To be fair to modern Protestants, this belief has been somewhat adapted to recognise that, though the elect may of course fall from time to time, they generally avoid serious crimes and sins.

The radical Protestant view that we are all "dung hills covered in snow," rather than a hierarchy of the saints in future heavenly glory, ranged about God, His angels and His saints, was the beginning of modern egalitarianism which eschews all idea of hierarchy and considers all men absolutely equal (and, under Protestantism, equally bad). It was also the beginning of that modern republicanism which eschews hierarchy and extols egalitarianism, since it regarded all true Protestants as already equally "saved" and thus already "saints," even in this life here below.

Hence Calvin's Genevan republic was called a "republic of saints" and, in England, the Puritans, after treacherously executing King Charles I, called their new republican assembly the "Parliament of Saints." Some "saints" these, that had just murdered their own King!

This "Parliament of Saints" was preceded by the "Rump" Parliament which consisted of those Members left after the Long Parliament was "purged," on 6 December 1648, by Colonel Thomas Pride, in "Pride's purge," throwing out all Members, many of them Presbyterians, who wanted the return of King Charles I or who were opposed to the execution of the King. This was done on the orders of Commissary General Thomas Ireton whose title and position have resonances with those of a Soviet commissar. Between 6 and 12 December 1648, Colonel Pride, supported by two regiments, prevented 231 Members from entering the House of Commons and imprisoned forty-five of them, so that the Army controlled the House entirely. The remaining Members, almost all extreme radicals, formed the "Rump" Parliament and voted to set up a bogus High Court to try the King which the House of Lords then rejected. Nevertheless, it was illegally set up. The King, upon being brought before it, accordingly challenged its jurisdiction. However, that illegal "court" then signed the King's death warrant and the King's execution proceeded soon after on 30 January 1649. Thereafter, the "Rump" Parliament voted to abolish both the House of Lords and the monarchy and established a Council of State to rule the new republic of Britain. Soon enough, Oliver Cromwell came to regard the "Rump" Parliament as corrupt and, on 20 April 1653, famously harangued them and said, in a speech no king would ever have dared to make, "Depart, I say; and let us have done with you. In the name of God, go!" He then declared "you are no Parliament" and called in a troop of soldiers, under the command of Major-General Thomas Harrison, ordering them to clear the chamber. Turning to the Speaker's Mace, the symbol of parliamentary power, he declared it a "fool's bauble" and ordered it taken away. Within a month he had set up a "Nominated Assembly" called "the Parliament of Saints." The absurdly named Puritan, Praise-God Barebone, leather seller, preacher, and member of the heretical millennialist sect the Fifth Monarchy Men, gave his name to this "Parliament of Saints," it being also called Barebone's Parliament. This "Parliament of Saints" came into being on 4 July 1653 and was the last attempt at political stability by the republic before the dictatorship called "the Protectorate." Cromwell and the Army Council nominated all its members (129 from England, five from Scotland, and six from Ireland, the latter all English army officers) so that it has appeared to posterity as a kind of proto-Fascist republican parliament. It dissolved itself, after much infighting, on 12 December 1653, and Cromwell, as "Lord Protector," then became dictator of the republic, a fate so often reserved for egalitarian, secularist republics throughout history.

The Puritan republics were the first secularist republics endorsing the principle of separation of Church and State (from which Puritan principle the United States gets its constitutional idea of a "wall of separation between Church and State," a principle that is now used to arrest harmless people praying outside abortion clinics).

The idea of a marriage of Church and State is a profoundly Catholic idea, being neither secularist, like most modern republics, nor theocratic, like many Islamic states, but a dyarchy as taught by Pope St Gelasius I, in his letter to the Eastern emperor, Anastasius I Dicorus, entitled *Famuli Vestræ Pietatis*. The latter is sometimes referred to as *Duo Sunt*, meaning "there are two," that is, two powers, spiritual and temporal, papal and imperial, by which the world is ruled, of which the higher is the spiritual.

This dyarchical idea was abandoned by many of the Protestant rebels but not, by any means, all. Thus, in England, King Henry VIII, who still considered himself a Catholic even after he had repudiated the Holy See, retained a form of dyarchical government but made the temporal ultimately superior to the spiritual.

This dyarchical marriage of Church and State is still the basis of our British Constitution and part of what makes us, at least nominally, a Christian constitutional monarchy, even if the State Church is Anglican and not Catholic and even if the temporal is unnaturally made superior to the spiritual.

However, the progress of the Protestant revolt in Britain later proceeded along very different and very unstable lines leading ultimately to civil war. It ended with the illegal execution and murder of King Charles I and the establishment of a unitary republic over England, Scotland, Ireland, and Wales, of which Oliver Cromwell would eventually become dictator as "Lord Protector."

The monarchy was restored in 1660 with King Charles II who was, in turn, succeeded by his younger brother, King James II of England and Ireland and VII of Scotland, who had converted to Catholicism.

Anti-Catholics, Puritans, and republicans, and those who had been revolutionaries under King Charles I, got up a petition to exclude the Catholic James, Duke of York, from the throne. They were called "Petitioners" or "Exclusionists" and were later called "Whigs." Those who abhorred the idea of Parliament seeking to exclude the rightful king from his rightful throne were called "Abhorrers" and were later called "Tories." From these origins came the two main political parties in the UK, the Liberal Party ("Whig") and the Conservative Party ("Tory").

King James II & VII, whilst remaining Catholic, was also Supreme Governor of the Church of England and, as King of Scots, royal protector of the Kirk, the Presbyterian Church of Scotland, and was thus naturally inclined to what we now call "ecumenism." In 1687 and 1688, he issued a Declaration of Indulgence granting religious liberty to all his subjects of any mainstream religion, including the heavily persecuted Catholics, and even, technically, Jews and Muslims.

Seven bishops, in a petition, refused to read the Declaration of Indulgence from the pulpit (the media of the day), considering it an affront to the state religion of Anglicanism, and so the King charged them with seditious libel. However, the King lost the case[3] and the seven bishops were acquitted. The King

---

3 *Dominus Rex versus Archiepiscopum Cantuariensem et al. De Termino Sanctæ Trinitatis Anno Regni Jacobi Secundi Regis, Quarto,* in Banco Regis,

was then betrayed by a conspiracy of civil and military officers and Anglican bishops, who feared that such a widespread grant of religious liberty would weaken the Church of England (and the Church of Scotland) which might, in turn, weaken their own privileged positions and wealth.

Some even feared, irrationally, that King James might demand that they return the stolen and looted monastery lands that their Protestant ancestors had seized. This was irrational because King James was in no position to do so and, moreover, had already promised not to do so.

Thus, these conspirators supported a foreign invasion from the Dutch Calvinist republic under the *Stadtholder*, Prince William of Orange, who invaded England on 5 November 1688 landing at Torbay, Devon. A treacherous part of King James's army then deserted their posts on Salisbury Plain and went over to William of Orange which turned the tide in the latter's favour. King James was forced to flee, having been deserted by officers like John Churchill, 1st Earl, and later 1st Duke, of Marlborough, ancestor of Sir Winston Churchill. William of Orange then became King William of England, Scotland, and Ireland. Savage penal laws against Catholics and "dissenters" were again restored by law and widened and magnified.

This event is known to history as the so-called "Glorious Revolution" of 1688, and with it the constitutions of England, Scotland and Ireland changed dramatically. It effectively made Parliament, instead of the King, sovereign. This was encapsulated in the so-called "Bill of Rights" of 1688 (which, despite being called a "bill" is, in fact, an Act of Parliament).

Thereafter, the circumstances in which the King could act alone, using the Royal Prerogative,[4] became severely limited.

Ironically, five of the seven acquitted bishops were subsequently removed from office by Parliament for refusing to swear allegiance to William of Orange. Despite their earlier hostility to

---

Die Veneris Decimo Quinto Die Junii, 1688 (The King v the Archbishop of Canterbury and others, in Trinity Term in the fourth year of the reign of King James II, in the Court of Kings Bench, on Friday 15 June 1688).
4   The Royal Prerogative is so called because it refers to the right of the King to speak (i.e., legislate or command) before (and after) all others, including Parliament. It comes from the Latin words *rogare*, to speak, and *pre-*, meaning "before," that is, *prerogare*: "to speak before" all others.

the Declaration, they considered William a usurper and not the true king and so refused to swear, remaining loyal to the king whom they had earlier resisted, King James II & VII. This was not, however, inconsistent but was in conformity with their belief in hereditary royal legitimacy. Instead, they formed a schismatic "non-juring" Anglican Church which later became the inspiration of the "High Church" and the Oxford Movement, the latter famously producing Cardinal St John Henry Newman. The non-jurors enjoyed good relations with the Episcopal Church of Scotland (ousted by the Presbyterians in 1637) and are, in a sense, the spiritual ancestors of the worldwide Anglican-Catholic Ordinariate.[5]

After the Bill of Rights 1688, what was left of the Royal Prerogative, now very severely curtailed, began to be whittled down more and more over the succeeding decades and centuries. From once having the power to prorogue Parliament whenever he did not need its advice (Parliament then being considered a body that advised the King, not one that dictated to him), the monarch could now not even refuse a bill presented to him for Royal Assent.

Today, the most important Prerogative powers are exercised *exclusively* by ministers and include the power to make war and deploy the armed forces, to conduct foreign policy and make treaties, to make public and judicial appointments, to issue passports, and to grant pardons and honours, among other powers.

The monarch still exercises some Prerogative powers himself, known as "the Reserve Powers" or "the personal Prerogatives" but, even then, only on the advice of ministers. The most important of these are the power to appoint and dismiss ministers, including the Prime Minister, to summon and prorogue parliament, and to give the so-called "Royal Assent" to bills passed by Parliament. However, all of these powers can *only* be exercised solely on the advice of ministers and not at the discretion of the monarch acting alone.

If there is concern that ministers have improperly advised the use of Prerogative powers, then the advice upon which these powers were exercised can, so the law now says, be reviewed by the

---

5 All of these non-jurors remained, unsurprisingly, the strongest supporters of the Catholic Stuart dynasty and of the Catholic Prince Charles Edward Stuart, "Bonnie Prince Charlie," particularly during the Jacobite uprisings to restore the legitimate Stuart dynasty to the thrones of England, Scotland, and Ireland.

courts[6] and thus, in effect, so can the exercise of those powers. Otherwise, they are unimpeachable by the courts.

Parliament itself can also overrule certain Prerogative powers by enacting a statute. For example, the power to appoint and regulate civil servants was placed on a statutory footing by the Constitutional Reform and Governance Act 2010 which also codified the constitutional convention that new treaties have to be laid before Parliament before the government can ratify them.

The very last time that a monarch refused Royal Assent to a bill was in 1708 when Queen Anne, the last of the Royal Stuarts (allowed by Parliament to accede to the throne because she was a Protestant), refused assent to the Scottish Militia Bill. However, she did so on the advice of her ministers, not on her own initiative.

It remains thus to this day. Under the British Constitution, the monarch may not refuse assent to any bill unless advised to do so by his ministers.

Indeed, the procedure today for giving Royal Assent usually involves Lords Commissioners, nominally appointed by the monarch, but, in fact, "on advice" of ministers (and thus actually appointed by the Prime Minister). They call upon the clerk of the House of Lords to signify the Royal Assent with the words "*Le Roy le veult*," meaning, in Law French, "the King wishes it," and the clerk duly speaks those words openly in the House. However, the monarch has, in reality, almost nothing to do with it.

However, the general view of constitutional lawyers is that there is one exception to the general rule that the monarch cannot veto a bill passed by Parliament and it is this: the monarch may refuse Royal Assent, and so veto a bill *against* or *without* the advice of ministers, if it is a bill that attempts permanently to destroy democracy by, for example, extending the life of Parliament indefinitely or by gerrymandering the electorate so that the government can never be removed. In short, the monarch has the power, right, and duty to protect democracy from a tyrant, dictator, or usurper who intends, like a Hitler or a Stalin, to destroy it. This is the one time the monarch may refuse Royal

---

6 A recent example of this was the 2019 prorogation ruling in which the Supreme Court decided that Mr Boris Johnson's advice to the Queen to prorogue parliament for five weeks was unlawful—see *R (Miller) v the Prime Minister* and *Cherry v Advocate General for Scotland* [2019] UKSC 41.

Assent, and so veto a bill, acting on his own discretion and even *against* the advice of ministers. The monarch is permitted so to do obviously because ministers are not going to advise vetoing their own attempt to abolish democracy. This is the one and only rare exception where the monarch may veto a bill on his own discretion, but it is a vital exception for obvious reasons.[7]

For similar reasons, the monarch also has power, acting alone on his own discretion, to dismiss a prime minister who refuses to resign after losing the confidence of the House of Commons.

In all other respects, however, the monarch has no more power to veto a bill passed by Parliament than do any of his subjects. If the monarch were to attempt to seize such a veto power, he would be subverting and destroying the very Constitution that he had sworn to uphold and protect. It would, in effect, be a *coup d'état* by the King against the State and thus a form of immoral and illegal sedition which St Thomas Aquinas condemns as seriously sinful.[8] If the present King were to try to do so then he, Charles Mountbatten-Windsor, would, in his private and personal capacity, be raising a rebellion against both Parliament and the Crown, that is, against King Charles III in his official capacity. It would be hard to imagine a more seriously illegal and immoral sedition than that.

St Thomas also teaches us that "accordingly the sin of sedition is first and chiefly in its authors, who sin most grievously."[9] The Church teaches the same.[10] It is also the teaching of the Catholic Church that the ends do not justify the means and that we may not do evil that good may come of it. Fimister, himself, says so in his *Voice of the Family* article: "so must we never do evil that good may come of it." This is also expressly taught by St Paul in Romans 3:8.[11]

Therefore, the monarch may not raise a sedition or a *coup d'état* in order to veto a bill that he has no power to veto, no matter how bad that bill may be. That would be "to do evil that good may come of it," the very thing that Fimister agrees we, as Christians,

---

7   See references in note 3 on page 6.
8   St Thomas Aquinas, *Summa Theologiæ*, II-II, q. 42.
9   Ibid., q. 42, a. 2.
10 *Catechism of the Catholic Church*, nos. 2238–40.
11 "And not rather (as we are slandered, and as some affirm that we say) 'let us do evil, that there may come good?,' whose damnation is just" (Rom 3:8).

may never do. Yet Fimister condemns our late Queen for not doing so—for not doing evil that good may come of it. He complains of "her complicity in the various immoral Acts of Parliament which disfigured her reign," failing to understand that she had no such "complicity" whatsoever because she had no such power.

As a matter of constitutional convention and law, Fimister is simply wrong. He has failed to understand that, under the British Constitution, it is Parliament that is sovereign, not the monarch, like it or not. To accuse our late Queen of sinning by refusing to veto the Abortion Bill (or any other immoral bills) one must first prove that she had such a power. However, as a matter of law, no such power belonged to her. One simply cannot blame a person for failing to exercise a power that the person does not possess.

The blame for these immoral bills must lie where it belongs: with those who *did* have power to pass them, namely the ministers and Parliament. To blame the Queen for them is, itself, a sin against charity, justice, and filial piety. It is like the bad policeman who, unable to catch the real criminal, arrests innocent people instead, and locks them up out of anger at not finding the true criminal. It is like the bad soldier who, unable to defeat the enemy and take a certain defended locality, takes out his anger on innocent local civilians by attacking them instead.

The British monarch is "sovereign" in name only. The true sovereign is Parliament. That is the meaning of the principle of parliamentary sovereignty.

Accordingly, the rest of Fimister's criticisms of our late Queen fall away.

Our late Queen was truly a model of unblemished character, virtue, selflessness and of Christian leadership, witness, and dignity, albeit as a Protestant. Britons were extremely fortunate to have her as head of state and for so many years. Very few heads of state can be compared to her in virtue and example. Those who wish to challenge or criticise our late Queen should first of all find out the true facts and not proceed from a position of unlearned error.

Catholics, in particular, should not cheapen themselves by carelessly and wrongly lashing out at her, and her seventy years of unimpeachable good conduct and good witness, by seeking to blame her for evils that she had no part in.

4

"Be not afraid of your office": The Monarch and Cooperation with Evil

Joseph Shaw

O NE OF THE COMPLAINTS CONSTANTLY heard from Catholics about the British monarchy, particularly from those Catholics less familiar with the constitutional conventions surrounding it, is that successive monarchs have failed either to prevent or to dissociate themselves from various bad laws: the Abortion Act of 1967, for example.

In this volume James Bogle explains in some detail why the concept of "Royal Assent" should not be confused with any action of the monarch which the monarch could withhold at will so as to veto a piece of legislation, and why the option of a temporary abdication, as done by King Baudouin of Belgium in 1990 in order to avoid signing a law authorising abortion, was not available to Queen Elizabeth. Furthermore, unlike an American President faced with a law he does not like which he cannot veto (his power to veto not being unlimited), a British monarch cannot even make a public protest about it, since by the most stringent constitutional convention, the monarchy must be publicly apolitical, like judges and civil servants.

These objectors, hearing this explanation, might respond as follows. Supposing it is impossible for the British monarch to prevent or even protest about bad legislation which is being promulgated, in some sense, in his name—or at least, in the name of the Constitution of which he is at the apex—would it not be better for a conscientious monarch to abdicate, permanently, in order to avoid cooperating with evil?

This chapter is an attempt to engage with this, second, objection. What I want to show is that the moral liceity of cooperating with evil is not just part of the Catholic tradition, but that it is fundamental to a Catholic conception of politics and of the moral life: a conception in which the Catholic statesman is not just allowed, but encouraged, to deal with the messy complexities of imperfect institutions and policies, while maintaining very clear boundaries about what he may and may not do.

COMMANDS TO DO EVIL

St Thomas More was a well-known public figure, and it would be reasonable to assume that his reputation for moral integrity was known to his executioner. It is possible that this individual was ideologically committed to the cause of King Henry VIII's divorce, and thought More's execution a good thing, but it is also very possible, and perhaps probable, that he had serious misgivings about it. Robert Bolt, in his well-known play about More, *A Man for All Seasons*, gives him this line, addressed to the headsman: "Friend, be not afraid of your office. You send me to God."

Here is a contrasting case. James Wolfe, the British general famous for his victories over the French in Quebec, was a young officer at the Battle of Culloden in 1746. The story is told that he was ordered by his commanding officer, the Duke of Cumberland, known as "Butcher Cumberland" (or more plausibly, by Cumberland's subordinate, Henry "Hangman" Hawley), to kill Charles Fraser of Inverlochy, who was found alive among the dead after the battle. Wolfe refused, saying "My commission is at your Highness's disposal, but I can never consent to become an executioner."[1]

Both of these stories may be apocryphal, but they illustrate important principles. What More seems to be saying to the executioner is that he is not acting wrongly in carrying out the sentence of death which had been passed against him. This judicial sentence was, of course, unjust, but it had the sanction of the law. The law under which More was prosecuted was itself unjust, but it had been passed with due form. As far as parliamentary procedure went, the law was the law; as far as juridical procedure went, the sentence of death was a sentence of death.

---

1 See John Prebble, *Culloden* (London: Folio Society, 1996), 93.

Wolfe, on the other hand, was being ordered by his superior to do an act which was illegal under the rules of war as understood at the time. However unlikely a prosecution against Wolfe in the circumstances might appear (unless the Jacobites had won after all), in principle the fact of his being commanded to carry out such an act would not have protected him. No one could imagine that the Duke of Cumberland had the authority to override the rules of war.

This, at any rate, seems to be the implication of the two stories. On a pacifist view, of course, all killing is wrong, but what the two stories are suggesting to us is a way of engaging with the complicated reality of killing under the law, which I shall call the classical view. On the classical view, then, public executioners, jailors, or soldiers ordered into battle may not know the justness of what they do, or they may have some dim understanding of it, but unless the injustice is very clear, they are not regarded as murderers or kidnappers. This is not because being ordered to do something by legitimate authority makes everything permissible, as the Wolfe story emphasises. It is because it is both unreasonable and impractical to expect the soldiers, executioners, jailors, and others to make moral judgements about some things, and not unreasonable or impractical to expect them to make moral judgments about other things, as when a legitimate superior makes a command egregiously beyond his authority.

Thus, the German soldiers ordered to invade Poland in 1939 were being asked to do something very seriously wrong: on the usual views of what justifies war, that war was not justified. Nevertheless, the classical view does not necessarily regard them as war criminals for that reason. Their information about the background to the war and the intentions with which it was undertaken was far from perfect, and they may have been very conscious of their limitations as judges of the justice of such vast geopolitical issues. It is not unreasonable for the ordinary soldier to leave such matters to his political leaders. Then again, no state could exist if every one of its servants decided for himself whether a particular commanded task was good or bad, and was allowed to refuse to act against his private opinion. The same is true for the exercise of authority within a private enterprise, in

44

the Church, or within a family. The notion of authority implies that the one exercising authority can *morally compel* subordinates to act: can create reasons for action which did not exist before, and in favour of which there is a strong presumption.

On the other hand, this does not mean everyone who has any kind of authority is elevated to the level of God. No court martial or human rights tribunal would punish a soldier for taking part in the wrongful invasion of another country, if the soldier did so in accordance with orders deriving from some recognisable legal authority. By contrast, the soldier will find no protection in a court or tribunal from any orders he may have received, for the act of (say) barricading a dozen women and children into a barn and burning them alive in it. Deliberately killing a dozen helpless non-combatants is not a *worse* crime than invading Poland, but it is *more clearly a crime*. It is clearly an act which no superior officer or supposed law could legitimate.

As I have explained it, this distinction depends on the psychology of the agent—the question of what it is reasonable to expect him to know, or to ask of him in terms of making moral judgements—as well as on the needs of government. Borderline cases are not difficult to imagine: a general, for example, privy to the aims of a war may see very clearly that it is unjust, even if his subordinates do not. Other difficult cases are thrown up by situations in which the legitimacy of the state can be called into question. I cannot explore these issues here. For present purposes it is sufficient to point out that even acts that appear to be intrinsically evil, such as executing an innocent man, can be carried out without guilt by those who are servants of an otherwise legitimate state. It is clear that this must be so for reasons deriving from the two sources I have stated: first, that the servant may have no access to the necessary facts, and may lack the psychological ability to make the necessary judgement; second, that no state could function unless there is at least a strong presumption in favour of the justness of its ordinances.

Heads of state, of course, are not commonly called upon to kill the innocent personally. Having established the above conclusion in that extreme case, the next thing to consider are cases where involvement with evil is more remote.

The Catholic conception of morality

Catholic moral theology is characterised by a very important distinction between intrinsically evil actions and other actions, which may be good or bad, that are nevertheless not intrinsically evil. An action is intrinsically evil, or evil *in itself* (*"per se"*), if it *aims* at an evil. If the death of an innocent person, or a bodily mutilation, or a sexual assault, or some other grave matter, is the *intention* of the action, then this is intrinsically evil. "Intention" and "aim" here should be understood in the normal sense, as what the agent is *trying to bring about.*

The reason people perform intrinsically evil actions is generally for some good result, or at least a result they regard as good. Even supposing this is a very great good, of more importance than the evil at issue, it does not justify the doing of an intrinsically evil action: that is the point of this category of action. Thus, if I could save five innocent lives by murdering one innocent person (at the insistence of a homicidal blackmailer, say, as in the plot of *The Pink Panther Strikes Again*), it would be wrong to do so.

This is not because we should always refuse to make comparisons between the outcomes of alternative possible actions. Supposing I were planning a famine relief effort, and calculated that I could save 1,000 lives in Region A if I established my camp there, while 500 lives would be lost in Region B; but that if I set up camp in Region B, the 500 lives would be saved there and the 1,000 lives lost in Region A. It is not heartless to work such things out, or to act on the conclusion: it is the right and proper thing to do. Such actions do not imply that the agents involved *aim at* the loss of lives which they, unfortunately, foresee. Where intrinsically evil actions are not at issue, we can fall back on choosing the *better* outcome, in terms of consequences. This is why the forbidding of certain actions as intrinsically evil has been called a system of "side-constraints":[2] it does not change the ultimate aim of one's actions, it simply sets limits to the legitimate means that can be adopted to achieve them.

However, while an official in charge of a famine relief effort naturally has the duty to minimise deaths, Catholic moral theology does not regard agents as being under a permanent obligation

---

2 Robert Nozick, *Anarchy, State and Utopia* (Oxford: Blackwell, 1974), 30.

to bring about the best possible outcome, even in the context of side-constraints. Instead, while the doing of intrinsically evil actions is forbidden, we are under a complex set of obligations, to family, state, Church, and community, none of which is normally all-consuming. It is usually possible, within this system, to use time and other resources in ways which are inefficient, in terms of the production of objective value: in leisure, for example.

However, there is another important component of the moral life that I have not yet mentioned, and that is the way that we can find ourselves cooperating with evil.

COOPERATION WITH EVIL

Aiming at an evil is intrinsically wrong, but many actions that do not aim at evil nevertheless bring evil results about, as in the example of famine relief given in the last section. As noted, it was not the *aim* of the agent in charge of the famine relief effort to bring about the death of the 500 people, but it is a consequence of his decision. The decision to establish the camp in Region A was the critical causal factor in the deaths of the 500 people in Region B. If the decision had gone the other way, those people would have been saved—at the cost of twice that number of people in the other region.

In other cases, we bring about evils, such as the deaths of innocent people, not merely by omission, but by action. Supposing I plan a new railway, calculating that if I divert one third of existing travellers between two cities from road to rail, I will save fifty lives a year from road accidents, while only five deaths a year would be likely on the railway. The calculation is a favourable one, but if I build the railway I will be causally responsible for the deaths of the five people a year. I foresee it, and by my actions I bring it about.

It is important to see the difference between this and the case of the *Pink Panther Strikes Again* noted earlier. As readers may recall, in this film a criminal mastermind with an obsessive hatred of Chief Inspector Clouseau threatens to destroy whole cities unless Clouseau is assassinated, and secret service agents of various countries accordingly attempt this. This of course is a farcical scenario, but the killing of individuals and groups, even of millions of people, for some supposed greater good, was all too common a feature of twentieth-century totalitarianism. In these historical examples the calculation that some great benefit would arise from the programme of mass-murder was itself absurd, even if those consumed by totalitarian ideology could not see this. However, on Catholic principles such a course of action would be wrong *even if it were true,* and demonstrably so, that some overwhelming good would result.

It is not wrong to bring about evils when this is *not* the intention, if in doing so this is proportionate to the good one is doing. It *is* wrong to bring about evils when this *is* the intention, even if this is going to bring about some much greater good.

The proponents of consequentialism (or utilitarianism) regard this as a morally arbitrary distinction, even a kind of superstition. Why, they ask, if it is possible foreseeably to *bring about* evils that good may come, is it not possible to *intend* evils that good may come? It is not possible to provide a full defence of the distinction in the context of this chapter, but I will point out the corruption of the agent which follows from a *focus* on evil: making evil one's *aim.* Once you set yourself to bring about something admittedly evil, however much you remind yourself that it is for a greater good, then you become an instrument of evil.

The contrast between a Catholic conception of the moral life, which is the same in structure to what is often called in academic ethics a "common sense" conception, and consequentialism, is of enormous importance. As I have explained it, it hinges not on whether we are allowed to compare anticipated outcomes or engage in prudential planning, but on what we as agents are allowed to make our aim. Bad results, possible or probable, attend every large-scale undertaking, and we should minimise them: on that we can agree with the consequentialist, though without making ourselves slaves of the idea that we should always bring about the best possible outcome. What we cannot do, even for the best imaginable outcome, is the intention of evil.

COOPERATION WITH EVIL
AND COLLECTIVE ACTION

In looking at the application of these principles, the case of the monarch is a special case of public servants in general, and these are not so very different from those involved in any kind of collective enterprise. Not only do our personal actions have evil consequences that we may be able to foresee, but we are involved in a more remote way with the evils that arise from the activities of the collective, to which we contribute.

Thus, as an employee of a company, not only are there evils that I am able to foresee from my personal actions performed in my role, but by supporting the company, by performing any action contributing to its efficiency and continued existence, from sweeping the floor to filing the accounts, I am helping to sustain the necessary conditions for the effectiveness of bad actions that may be performed by my colleagues or superiors. It is difficult to think of bad foreseen direct consequences of sweeping the floor, but a clean and tidy workplace contributes to the efficiency of the firm, and if the firm is doing something bad—such as per-forming abortions, to take an extreme case—the cleaner is, in a small way, contributing to that.

I have been talking about evils that are not intended, and the Catholic tradition calls involvement with these "material cooper-ation," as opposed to the "formal cooperation" of intending the evil. Leaving formal cooperation aside, material cooperation can be close (or "proximate"), or it can be remote. Handing a known mass-murderer ammunition would be close, even if it is not formal (even if the agent does not intend the murders); sweeping the floor of an abortion clinic is remote, because it is connected with the evil only by a long chain of causes, is not a major contribution to the actions immediately bringing about the evil, and so on.

What is true of a private enterprise is true of one's involvement with the state. The effectiveness of a state is aided by all the small and great acts of cooperation, not only of its employees and officers, but of its citizenry. The vast machine of the modern state does all kinds of good things, and also all kinds of bad things, including, routinely, the killing of the innocent in the womb. The question of cooperation with evil in this context is a particularly difficult one.

The manualist tradition—the tradition of manuals of Catholic moral theology used in Catholic seminaries in the century and more up to the mid-twentieth century—makes a useful if inexact distinction between the kinds of action we must take in response to close and to remote material cooperation with evil. It says that we should be prepared to undergo "grave inconvenience" to avoid close cooperation, but that this is not necessary to avoid remote cooperation. It should be noted that close material cooperation with evil is not itself intrinsically evil: that is the whole point of the distinction made above about what constitutes intrinsically evil actions. It can, then, be justified, and in the very short term it may be necessary to protect one's livelihood, to sustain one's children, and the like. Nevertheless, close cooperation with evil is something that should be avoided, and we should go to some trouble to avoid it, otherwise we are guilty of sin.

This is not so of remote cooperation with evil. Certainly, we should avoid it when to do so is easy: if there is no, or minimal, inconvenience. But we are not under an obligation to take on grave inconvenience to do so. This is not because the manualists want to be soft on people; it is because remote material cooperation with evil is *everywhere*. This in turn is not because—or not only because—of the uniquely bad state of modern society; it is because, as I have underlined in my examples, it is unavoidable even when undertaking laudable projects. Bad things happen whenever you do good; join with others to do a great good, and the bad side-effects will multiply. This is not to say that they necessarily outweigh the good to be done: if they did, then the project would be a bad idea. They will multiply even if they are vastly outweighed by the good results, and even if all reasonable steps have been taken to minimise them.

In the Catholic moral tradition we are obliged to make continual judgements about our involvement in all kinds of collective projects—commercial firms, political parties, the state—as to whether we are cooperating with evil, whether this is close or remote, whether it can be avoided easily or only with grave inconvenience, and what the alternatives might be. The Catholic conception of the moral life means that we remain aware of these evils, and do not regard them as of no account, and that we always seek ways to minimise them or, if that is impossible, to distance ourselves from them. At the same time, it does not create the paralysis of someone who sees the evil associated with every possible option, and horrified by this, can see no way to act.

For the alternative to the Catholic approach, which might present itself as more highminded, the view that says that all cooperation with evil should be avoided regardless of the cost, would indeed lead to paralysis. Even staying in bed all day or fleeing to the hills would not free one from cooperation with evil, since cooperation can be done as well by omission, as by action. A useful traditional list of forms of cooperation with evil found in Catholic examinations of conscience ("Nine Ways to Participate in Another's Sin")[3] includes "silence," when some wrong has been done, and our failure to protest or take other action is a contribution to it. We might add to that the owning of shares in a company that does evil, buying the products or using the services of such firms, or having as a customer of one's own enterprise an individual who brings evil about. There is literally no way of feeding and clothing oneself, let alone a way of earning money, that does not involve remote material cooperation with evil.

The entirely fictitious project of purifying oneself from all cooperation with evil gives way, in the Catholic conception of the moral life, to a willingness to deal with the world as we find it, that all the same never stops caring about the evils, however inevitable they may seem, and resolutely refuses to become their instrument by intention.

CONCLUSION

The purpose of this chapter, as noted at the beginning, is to explore the question of cooperation with evil once the idea that the monarch has direct control over the promulgation of bad laws has been set aside. *Even then*, the objector may say, the unique place of the monarch in the political system makes it intolerable for him to remain there when the state does something really bad.

There may, indeed, be situations in which a monarch may feel obliged to abdicate in protest. This will depend very much on the nature of the constitutional system and the political circumstances. However, though the state brings about bad things every day, it is very rarely the case that a Christian monarch could do more good than harm by abandoning his position, and as noted above, when we do not have to do with an intrinsically evil action, we must consider the balance of harms. It may make for a more

---

3   This list is found, for example, in Q. 329 of *The Penny Catechism or A Catechism of Christian Doctrine, Approved by the Archbishops and Bishops of England and Wales, and Directed to be Used in All Their Dioceses* (1971), p. 55.

morally comfortable life to escape involvement in constitutional affairs, but it would almost certainly be to the detriment of the people, whom the monarch has sworn to serve: to serve, above all, as I argue in chapter 14, as a sacred symbol.

This would not just be an action that contributed to an evil through material cooperation. It would involve something I have not mentioned in this chapter: the breaking of a positive duty created by the oath of office.

5

Lost Dignity: On the Dignified Aspect of Government and the Problem of Totalitarianism

SEBASTIAN MORELLO

I N 1868, THE LEARNED ESSAYIST WALTER Bagehot published his series on *The English Constitution* in a single volume of that name. The appetite during the nineteenth century for some account of our constitution resulted in a mixed blessing. The English Constitution had been traceable in written documents such as the Magna Carta (1215), the Bill of Rights (1687), and the Acts of Union (1707); it was observable in concrete institutions such as the monarchy, the two Houses of Parliament, and the Inns of Court; and it was detectable in approaches we customarily took to resolving problems: the common law system, representative democracy embodied in an MP, and a shared culture. What the Constitution *is*, however, and what *is* and what *isn't* an essential component of it, was always left ambiguous. The great constitutional lawyers, from Sir John Fortescue in the fifteenth century to Erskine May in the nineteenth, hadn't entirely agreed on the nature of the Constitution and its essential content. Thus, like the Constitution itself, the analysis of it took the form of an ongoing conversation, and in any case the Constitution was widely felt to be based upon various unspoken assumptions and "ways of thinking and doing things," as it has commonly been said.

There is a reason why an inordinate desire to understand inherited things, especially the structures and constitutions of nations,

53

had emerged in the preceding eighteenth century, just as a frenzy arose for wrecking nations and seeking to author new ones *ex nihilo*: it is very difficult to destroy that which remains a mystery. Once something is known, grasped, and its essential parts understood, it may be deconstructed and reconfigured for ideological purposes by meddlers and destroyers (as we witnessed playing out during the turn of the most recent century with the constitutional meddling of Prime Minister Tony Blair). One of the principal components that made the English Constitution so resilient and successful was the fact that it was deemed something of an organically unfolding mystery, about which people thought very little—at least in any abstract or rationalistic way—whilst simultaneously always depending upon its life, like the leaves on an ancient oak.

Bagehot's work on the English Constitution was an immediate success, and it was instrumental in developing Victorian self-understanding regarding what it was to belong to these Isles. Part of the achievement of this work was that it sought to avoid an overly abstract account of the Constitution. Indeed, Bagehot declared from the outset that he wasn't interested in proposing a *theory* (what he termed a "paper description") to explain the Constitution, but instead would concentrate on the actual and existent centres of power and how the political system practically operated—what he called the "living reality." A crucial theme of Bagehot's account was that there were two chief components to government in the English system, which he termed the "efficient" and the "dignified" aspects of government.

Monarchy: the dignified aspect of government *par excellence*

In the various centres of power, the government's efficient and dignified aspects—what Bagehot termed "parts"—are admixed. Whilst Bagehot notes that the two Houses of Parliament are predominantly *efficient*, being those centres of power by which the government "in fact, works and rules," they also have a certain dignified character of their own—expressed by their special garments and ceremonies—which is meant to inspire reverence both in their offices' incumbents and in those subject to their power. So too, whilst the monarchy is deemed by Bagehot to be chiefly part of the *dignified* aspect of government, whose main role is to stir patriotic loyalty in the population, the monarchy is nonetheless understood to possess a degree of efficient control, if only in its remaining veto-power (namely, the power to reject any attempt by Parliament to pass an act that would end democracy in these Isles).

For Bagehot, the monarchy is the summit of the dignified aspect of government, and its foremost benefit is found in the domain of "feelings." "The characteristic of the English Monarchy," wrote Bagehot, "is that it retains the feelings by which the heroic kings governed their rude age, and has added the feelings by which the constitutions of later Greece ruled in more refined ages."[1] It is precisely the monarchy's capacity to conserve the feelings of national loyalty *through* transformations of government down the ages that gives it the character of perennial value.

This "perennial value" is surely what makes monarchy—quite apart from its sacral origins—so bound up with religious sentiment. As Bagehot writes:

> The English Monarchy strengthens our government with the strength of religion. It is not easy to say why it should be so. Every instructed theologian would say that it was the duty of a person born under a republic as much to obey that republic as it is the duty of one born under a monarchy to obey the monarch. But the mass of the English people do not think so; they agree with the oath of allegiance; they say it is their duty to obey the "Queen," and they have but hazy notions as to obeying laws without a queen.[2]

The principle here is a simple one. It is difficult to see how a man placed in power by the will of the people may possess any lasting authority among them, since he possesses his power by the authorship of those he governs. Moreover, how can he personally enjoy the deep loyalty of a people who will soon see him exchanged for another? A democratically elected leader is not a father of the nation, but a visitor to governmental power who will disappear as quickly as he appeared. He has not ascended to his seat by way of the providential unfolding of a dynasty whose origins are lost in the ages of mythology, but he has ascended by the impulses of those no different from himself.

---

1   Walter Bagehot, *The English Constitution*, no. III "The Monarchy," art. 1.
2   Ibid.

It is the common experience of man that democratic and republican government normally possesses neither the sacral character nor the existential dignity to capture the affections of the people. Indeed, such political arrangements invariably arise out of rebellion and irreverence towards settled politics, simultaneously legitimating all future rebellion and irreverence. The failure of such systems to inspire affection in their citizenry can be seen in the American republic, where it has been necessary increasingly to transform the US President into a monarchical figure, who now not only demands an extraordinary depth of devotion but possesses power that sacral monarchs of the old continent could only have dreamed of. The jury is out, of course, on how long that state of affairs can last—indeed, the cracks are very much already visible.

A document or a flag will never be able to inspire the affections among a people that monarchy can effect in a nation. The reason for this is that a monarch is a *person*, and so the species of political affection in this case is *interpersonal affection* (this sort of warmth towards a nation *embodied in a person* was on full display to the whole world during the national mourning and funeral ceremonies for Queen Elizabeth II at the end of 2022). A man may pledge allegiance to a flag or an emblem or a written document, but such things have not pledged allegiance to him, and he may sensibly remain suspicious of any interpreters of such symbols. In the case of monarchy, one may not only be moved by loyalty to the monarch but reasonably believe that the monarch is moved by loyalty to his subjects. Given that it is precisely by *interpersonal relatedness* that we flourish (which is why we form political societies at all), a government centred on this deepest aspect of human nature is surely incalculably more robust than any government that centres loyalty on an impersonal object.

PATRIOTISM AND THE
DIGNIFIED ASPECT OF GOVERNMENT

The point of Bagehot's bipartite distinction of the *efficient* and *dignified* aspects of government is as follows: any successful government must be capable of *moving* the nation's members both from without and from *within*. The nation's members are moved from without by means of law and regulation and the coercive enforcement of such. The nation's members are moved from within by patriotic feeling and national loyalty. There is a tendency among modern people to dismiss the latter as being of no importance, seeing the dignified aspect of government as mere "window dressing" and treating efficient government as the only aspect of any consequence. This is a grave mistake.

When a government cannot rely on the loyalty and patriotic feeling of its citizenry, it quickly depends more on coercion to maintain order and civil stability—the procurement of which is its job. As a sense of patriotism wanes, so too must the state grow increasingly invasive and intrusive, as it can no longer rely on its citizens to be "moved from within" for the good of the nation as a whole. This is largely why conservative governments prize patriotism and treat excessive statism as unnecessary if patriotism is properly fostered, and why liberal and progressive governments peddle national repudiation whilst escalating the emergence of a highly coercive surveillance state. Admittedly, there is a liberal tradition of nationalist emotion—especially exhibited in the revolutionary upheavals of 1789 and 1848—but such nationalism was always a means to increased statism and political expansionism. The liberal anthropology of atomisation will always remain in tension with patriotic feeling; and thus, for the liberal, order and stability will be maintained by Leviathan alone. No such dilemma, however, arises from the conservative's communitarian anthropology.

The English can take pride in the fact that the dignified aspect of their government isn't founded on a mere "noble lie." Rather, it principally comprises an ancient sacral monarchy, regenerated with each monarch, beginning with an anointing from a lord spiritual (a bishop)—a venerable institution that has come down through the ages with the destined rise of an island people. Through centuries of oscillating between violence and negotiation, they have found a beautiful way to belong together, and every facet of their government's dignified aspect testifies to this work of providence.

As the philosopher Simone Weil pointed out in *The Need for Roots*, the French are condemned to conjure up a sense of loyalty from a *lie*—and hardly a noble one—that theirs is a nation born from an "Enlightenment" dream of universal fraternity, freedom, and equality. Theirs, they must hold, is a nation that sprang forth from a piece of paper as if by magic, whose sorcery required nothing more than the crushing of religion and the murder of their own people—a small sacrifice for the miracle of "the Republic." The English, thankfully, must subscribe to no such fiction. Indeed, the English remain one of the few peoples left on earth who may claim to live under a *noble truth*, albeit one hampered by accumulated Whiggish myths which now have the upper hand in their land's current condition of decay.

THE DIGNIFIED ASPECT OF GOVERNMENT AND THE PROBLEM OF TOTALITARIANISM

Edmund Burke, in his *Reflections on the Revolution in France*, pointed out that as patriotism fades with what he called the emergence of "cold hearts," law and order necessarily become increasingly dependent both on "terrors" and the citizenry's motivation by private interest to do what is right:

> On the scheme of this barbarous philosophy, which is the offspring of cold hearts...laws are supported only by their own terrors, and by the concern, which each individual may find in them, from his own private speculations, or can spare to them from his own private interests. In the groves of *their* academy, at the end of every vista, you see nothing but gallows. Nothing is left which engages the affections on the part of the commonwealth. On the principles of this mechanic philosophy, our institutions can never be embodied, if I may use the expression, in persons; so as to create in us love, veneration, admiration, or attachment. But that sort of reason which banished the affections is incapable of filling their place.... To make us love our country, our country ought to be lovely.[3]

With the successive undermining of the dignified aspect of government (though, of course, he didn't use that terminology), Burke sees a looming dependence on a diabolic combination of authoritarian and totalitarian government. The alternative he offers to such an arrangement is that of loyalty to the nation "embodied in persons." One cannot rely on constitutional mechanisms to prevent totalitarianism; rather, one must rely—to use Burke's

---

3 Edmund Burke, *Reflections on the Revolution in France* (London: Penguin Books, 1986), 171–72.

list—on the love, veneration, admiration, and attachment of a patriotic people. (As the late Professor Sir Roger Scruton noted in his memoirs, *Gentle Regrets*, it was less a hatred for Communism and more a love for the civilisation that Communism trampled that eventually enabled dissidents to topple that noxious regime.)

Burke concludes that "to make us love our country, our country ought to be lovely." This is a leading reason why conservatives see the wrecking of both the countryside and the urban environment as not only a pressing issue, but as *essentially* relevant to the question of what kind of political settlement we are going to find ourselves being governed by in the coming decades. Urban sprawl and ugly architecture aren't simply sources of tremendous suffering—as people increasingly struggle to see their country as a shared home—but they make the country itself *unlovable*, or at least far less lovable. And benign government requires that its citizenry love their national territory.

Paradoxically, then, the dignified aspect of government possesses an efficient power of its own—one, however, that is subtle and tacit—on which the efficient aspect of government depends to prevent it from overstepping its own mark. It is because conservatives believe that their country should be not just orderly but "lovely," and that its lovability prevents the encroachment of the sort of surveillance state that has now emerged to frustrate our lives, that they are prone to become incensed in the face of unworthy and corrupt ministers and the decline of accountability. Anything that diminishes patriotic affection among the nation's members is insufferable to conservative-minded people. So too, conservatives cannot endure royals undermining the dignity of the royal house, either by chaotic relationships or adoption of celebrity culture. Equally, however, they cannot exercise patience towards the critics of monarchy who have become so ubiquitous in the counterfeit culture that now dominates English society.

A government that allows, even facilitates, the desecration of its country's landscapes; that indulges in, encourages even, constant national self-repudiation; that develops no appropriate border policy, forcing its settled inhabitants to feel like strangers in a foreign land; that mocks and belittles expressions of patriotic sentiment: such a government isn't only leading the country towards national suicide but risks, in the meantime, placing

59

it on the highway to totalitarianism. In the UK, in 2018, over 3,300 people were arrested, detained, and questioned for opinions they'd posted on their social media accounts. This example alone suffices to reveal the trajectory of this country that risks ceasing, in Burke's words, "to be lovely." There is a solution to this terrible situation, but it is to be found in the unfashionable feelings of patriotism, gratitude, and national loyalty, for which the dignified aspect of government is so necessary.

II

THE
CORONATION

6

Coronation is a Ritual Humiliation

SOHRAB AHMARI

A T THE APPROACH OF THE CORONATION of King Charles and Queen Camilla, a subset of pro-gressive opinion could not help but vent disdain for the ancient ritual. The environmentalist campaigners entitled "Just Stop Oil" refused to rule out disruptive action (claiming that we are facing "civilisational collapse," after all).[1] A protester with the anti-monarchy group "Republic" told *ABC News*: "I think it's a disgrace. To think this country is in a mess, and we're spending out millions on a coronation."[2] A commentator from *The Guardian* newspaper sneered that if local cinemas showed the Coronation, it would mean "all the people who actually like that rubbish will all be in one place, and I'll be able to go about my day unimpeded."[3]

While such animus is out of step with mainstream opinion, it's clear that the Coronation has lost its romance and even its meaning among some of the wider public. Two-thirds of respon-dents tell *YouGov* pollsters that they either don't care very much or don't care at all about the ceremony. Only 9% of Britons said they care "a great deal," and that cohort tends to be elderly.[4]

Modern Britons may well ask: why do we find ourselves locked into a ritual—a religious ritual, to be precise—inherited from the ancient past? Even if some share the Christian faith that underpins rituals like the Coronation, can't they practise that faith privately, without the need for a solemn, state-sanctioned

---

1 Reported by *Metro*, 20 April 2023.
2 *ABC News*, 8 March 2023.
3 *The Guardian*, 27 April 2023.
4 *YouGov*, 13 April 2023, https://yougov.co.uk/topics/politics/survey-results/daily/2023/04/13/b7aff/1.

ceremony involving bishops, priests, crowns, sceptres, and holy oils? Why do we need public ritual at all?

All this failure to understand the meaning is a tragedy, because old rituals like the Coronation can play a deeply salutary—and even progressive—role in societies otherwise wracked by modern capitalism's cruel, arbitrary hierarchies. We human beings do all sorts of things that have no functional value in themselves but that help us communicate symbolically. We shake hands. We exchange rings. We are wired, it seems, for ritual: a pattern of words and actions characterised by formality, rigidity, and repetition. The closest analogous human behaviour, according to many anthropologists, is games.

In the middle of the last century, a husband-and-wife team of British anthropologists travelled to Africa in an attempt scientifically to understand the ritual process. Specifically, they sought the meaning of religious rites among traditional tribes; ultimately, it awakened them to the indispensability of ritual for decent and stable societies.

Victor Witter Turner was born in 1920 in Glasgow. As a teenager, under the tutelage of an Anglican priest, he was drawn to mystical traditions. But by the time "Vic" entered university and married, he had become a card-carrying Communist. His wife, "Edie," had also embraced Marxism early on, because it was, she said, a worldview "wrung clean of religion."

In the late 1940s, the couple discovered Margaret Mead's scholarly work *Coming of Age in Samoa* in a public library. It inspired Vic to study anthropology: he was thrilled by the thought of living hand-to-mouth in remote places, and drawn, too, to the "neat social systems among indigenous islanders" that seemed to exist "like an organism with its own socially structural laws." He worked under Max Gluckman, the legendary leader of the structural anthropology movement based at the University of Manchester, who dispatched Vic to central Africa to study "chieftainship politics."

Ritual, of course, was central to defining the individual's roles within the "neat social systems" in which he was interested. For example, many tribal peoples mark the passage from childhood to adulthood with highly elaborate rites, whereas in the modern West, childhood often merges imperceptibly with adulthood, leaving it to each individual to figure out what it means to "come of age."

Many anthropologists then dismissed tribal ritual as the unintelligible mumbo-jumbo of a "simpler" people. But in 1951, Gluckman sent Vic a telegram urging him to switch to researching the religious practices of the Ndembu people of south-central Africa. Edie came along. The Turners' time among the Ndembu convinced them that such supercilious attitudes were false. "In matters of ritual as of art," Vic would write years later in his seminal 1969 text, *The Ritual Process*,[5] "there are no 'simpler' peoples, only peoples with simpler technologies than our own. Man's imaginative and emotional life is always and everywhere rich and complex."

Zambia, where the Turners encountered these people, was then a British colony known as Northern Rhodesia. Nevertheless, the Ndembu welcomed the foreign couple's attempts to understand their rituals, even inviting them to participate. The Turners studied the *Isoma*, a rite that treated women suffering from infertility. The central action of the ritual involved the afflicted woman and her husband walking in the nude several times between two holes, one identified as "cold" and the other "hot," representing both the grave and the birth canal. In this way, the ritual reconciled the once-warring communities of the living and the dead.

The Dutch-German anthropologist Arnold van Gennep, whose ideas the Turners borrowed, taught that every rite involves three stages. First, a separation, when the subjects are removed from the social structure. Next, the liminal stage, when the subjects become indeterminate, ambiguous, outcast even: during the core action of the *Isoma*, the afflicted couple no longer occupy their symbolic roles as husband and wife; their nakedness signifies that they are more like newborns, or the dead. Finally, there is a reaggregation, when the subjects return to the social structure, either in a new condition—a boy emerges as a man after the extreme trials of the coming-of-age ritual—or merely restored to their prior condition—the afflicted couple now "healed" by *Isoma*.

The Turners focused their analysis on the middle stage. As Vic explained, liminal beings "are neither here nor there; they are betwixt and between the positions assigned and arrayed by

---

5 Victor Turner, *The Ritual Process: Structure and Anti-Structure* (Piscataway, NJ: Aldine Transaction, 1969).

law, custom, convention, and ceremonial." To become liminal is to assume a transcendent vulnerability; it is the condition of Christ on the Cross. The humiliation of the liminal subject, for the Turners, fostered *communitas*, a state apart from the structured hierarchies we inhabit most of our lives. *Communitas*, a primordial state beyond rank and class, reminds us that the high and mighty have their status only in relation to the low, and "he who is high must experience what it is like to be low."

Before he assumed power, a Ndembu chieftain had to undergo ritual humiliation at the hands of a mythic figure known as the *Kafwana*; coded female, she was associated with the land and the people who tilled it, those who weren't politically or militarily strong but who nevertheless possessed a sacral power. Among other things, the chieftain-to-be had to absorb a barrage of insults and criticisms from other villagers; once installed, he didn't dare hold it against the people. In this way, the religious ritual taught the chieftain that he was first and foremost a servant.

By humbling himself, and dispensing with his normal privileges, the one undergoing the ritual must recognise what Vic called "humankindness" that is "a generic bond between men." Without it, the hierarchical community has no qualms about excluding, and even destroying, the weak. Far from locking people into the past, then, ritual allows them to confront present and future challenges. Ritual, in this telling, humanises societies.

On the surface, the Coronation of King Charles and Queen Camilla is about as distant as can be from the chieftainship ritual of the Ndembu people. But the rite's underlying structures are shockingly similar. The Anglican ceremonial adds several layers of Christian symbolism, not to mention genteel ornamentation—all of which softens the liminal humiliation of the king-to-be and his bride—but the fundamental process is the same.

First, there is the separation of the ritual subjects—Charles and Camilla—from humdrum British reality. This is marked by their carriage ride to Westminster Abbey. Next comes the liminal stage, where Charles's face is literally covered by Anglican churchmen, using a canopy of golden cloth, or, for the 2023 ceremony, the "anointing screen." These coverings shield the most sacred element of the ritual from prying eyes, but it also means that Charles is erased as an individual.

The core action of the liminal stage is the anointing of the king's hands, breast, and head with oil. In the Bible, such oils are the mark of the self-sacrificing King of Kings: Jesus is anointed before he is to undergo his passion, death, and burial. Once the screen is removed, the anointed king will kneel at the high altar while the archbishop recalls how "Our Lord Jesus Christ, the Son of God...was anointed with the Oil of gladness above his fellows." Thus Charles, as a Christian statesman, is united with the sacrifice of Christ. He is giving up something, trading his personality for that of the sovereign, duty-bound to serve the *commonweal.*

Finally, there is Charles's reaggregation: he re-enters society with elevated status, symbolised by the crown and sceptre. But again, this occurs only after he has ritually identified himself with society's victims—indeed, with the anointed Victim of victims. All this marks him out as the servant-ruler of the British people, rather than merely a political leader.

Today's economic hierarchies tell the winners that they owe their status to no one and nothing but their own "meritocratic" efforts. This isn't, in fact, true: study after study demonstrates that social mobility has stalled, especially in the Anglosphere. But it makes for particularly obnoxious elites: if they owe their status to no one, then they also have no obligations to society's losers. Against such a backdrop, Britain's traditional monarchic rituals, not least the Coronation, are a very different, and much needed, account of what the high owes the low.

When we glimpse the *communitas* lying beyond everyday structures—when we leave behind profane, everyday reality to play the solemn, cosmic game of ritual—we are possessed by a vision of what society could or should look like. Here, the mighty chieftain submits to the lowly *Kafwana.* Here, the omnipotent Son of God consents to be humiliated. And his Majesty the King consents to follow the mortified God-man, even into the symbolic tomb.

7
An Eighth Sacrament?

CHARLES A. COULOMBE

O N 6 MAY 2023, KING CHARLES III WAS
crowned at Westminster Abbey—as almost every king
of England has been since William the Conqueror
went through a similar ceremony in 1066. The round of rituals
since his mother's death last year remind the informed observer
of just how much Catholic ceremonial has been retained by the
repurposed monarchy since the so-called Glorious Revolution of
1688. Leaving aside the controversy amongst Catholics that the
British monarchy inevitably arouses, it is ironic that the very flaws
many of us see in the institution are the result of an event which
is still considered part of the march of progress from Magna Carta
to the American Revolution and the Emancipation Proclamation
of 1863, freeing the nation's slaves. But let us leave all that alone
and look more closely at a ceremony that is in fact deeply rooted
in the Catholic view of governance that held sway at least until
1918—and as far as the papacy itself was concerned, 1963.

A great deal has been said about the alterations in the ceremony since it was last used in 1953 for Queen Elizabeth II, and
often enough used to criticise the new monarch for it all. But
the truth is that the LGBT and refugee choirs at the following
concerts, and the vaguely referenced alterations to the ceremony
itself are the doing not of the King but "his" government and his
"subjects." When his mother was crowned, Churchill was Prime
Minister and her peoples—especially in Britain and in the areas
briefly occupied by the Japanese—had just proved their bravery,
and, in the United Kingdom, were still under wartime rationing.
The Queen's coronation reflected them. His Majesty's governments
and peoples are far different from the embattled veterans (often
enough of two major wars) who hailed his mother.

One factoid that has in fact caught media attention has been the nature of the chrism with which the King was anointed as part of the ceremony; the pundits are excited that it was chrism obtained without cruelty to any animal. Apart from the suspicion that such an oil is like "Mountain-Grown Coffee" or "Sugar-free Petroleum"—a product that need not be mentioned—it is not the most important fact about the chrism at all. That fact is that, prepared in Jerusalem, it was co-consecrated by the Greek Orthodox Patriarch of Jerusalem, alongside the Anglican archbishop of the city. This means that for the first time since the coronation of King James II & VII in 1685, the Coronation chrism was indisputably blessed by a hierarch in the Apostolic Succession. It will then be a sacramental with certain blessings attached to it—regardless of the status of the "archbishop" who actually anointed the King with it at the Coronation (Catholics must consider him a clerically-clothed layman, unless he has the "Dutch Touch" of Old Catholic orders, as some Anglican bishops do).[1] But the fact that chrism is being used at all takes us back to England's Catholic past.

The anointing was the most sacred part of the Catholic coronation rite—even more than the placing of the crown upon the new monarch's head. This was so when Blessed Karl I was crowned King of Hungary in 1916, when Ferdinand of Austria was crowned King of Bohemia in 1838 and King of Lombardy-Venetia in 1836, when Charles X received the French Crown in 1830, and when Franz II was crowned Holy Roman Emperor in 1792—all the way back through successive emperors and kings to the early Middle Ages. It was seen as a renewal of the rite performed by Samuel for King David. This was an important sign and more than symbol for our Catholic ancestors. For them, kingship was participation in the Kingship of Christ—which participation was actualised by the Coronation, which gave the monarch authority to rule. The anointing for most monarchs was done with the oil of catechumens; but by papal permission, those of France, England, Scotland, Sicily, and Jerusalem were

---

1   This refers to episcopal consecration by schismatic "Old Catholic" or Jansenist bishops from the Netherlands, which was sought out by some Anglicans concerned to establish the validity of their orders following Leo XIII's negative judgement about them in his Bull *Apostolicæ Curæ* (1896).

done with chrism.[2] In short, the oil being prepared for King Charles—although blessed by a Greek Orthodox Patriarch for an Anglican rite—is what it is because of the popes—not unlike the King's title of "Defender of the Faith."[3]

Charles III's coronation followed the same basic structure and used most of the words and prayers of its Catholic prototype. The individual today called the "archbishop of Canterbury" officiated, in emulation of those prelates in Catholic times. In every Catholic realm, it was the Primate—Canterbury in England, Reims in France, Toledo in Castile, etc., that performed the rite, as the highest cleric in the country; but to the pope was reserved the coronation of the Holy Roman Emperor in Rome—just as, on a few occasions, they had crowned the Byzantine Emperor while visiting Constantinople.

The bishops of the Church of England and the British peers gathered in Westminster Abbey, even as was done before the Protestant Revolt. Then as now, the king would be recognised officially by these key officers in the State. Before them the new monarch would swear to defend the Church, and to maintain the people in their rights. Then, in every country where this rite was performed, the anointing followed. This very sacred element of the ceremony—resembling as it did extreme unction, due to the anointing of the head, chest, back, and elbow—led many commentators to refer to it as a sort of "eighth sacrament."

This impression was reinforced by the clothing that followed the imposition of the oil of catechumens or chrism. While varying according to country, most versions of the rite featured the monarch being clothed in garments reminiscent of diaconal vestments—stole, dalmatic, and so on. The Catholic king was considered to be a

---

2 The oil of catechumens is pure olive oil, and is used in the ceremony of baptism, before the baptism proper. The oil of chrism is olive oil mixed with balsam; it is considered more sacred, and used in the ceremony of baptism immediately after the baptism proper, and in confirmation, holy orders, and the consecration of a church.

3 *Fidei Defensor*: a title given to King Henry VIII by Pope Leo X in 1521 in recognition of his book attacking the theology of Martin Luther, *Assertio Septem Sacramentorum* ("Defence of the Seven Sacraments"). Despite the title being revoked after Henry's break with Rome, it has continued to be used on the authority of a 1543 Act of Parliament, and appears on British coins and elsewhere, often abbreviated to *"Fid. Def."*

"mixed person," partaking at once of lay and clerical character. As a result, the Holy Roman Emperor served as deacon and the king of France as subdeacon at papal Masses when in Rome—and the latter monarch, at his coronation, received from the chalice at Mass like a priest. If the emperor was visiting the pope at Christmas, he would sing a lesson from the Matins of Christmas Eve at St Peter's Basilica. In Rome, the Holy Roman Emperor was made a canon of St Peter's Basilica, the king of France was given a canonry of St John Lateran, and the kings of Spain and England (until the break with Rome) the same positions at St Mary Major and St Paul-Outside-the-Walls respectively: most Catholic monarchs (including this quartet) had various canonries and position in royal abbeys and other religious foundations.

The robing completed, the king or emperor was then presented with the sword of state; he would draw it from the scabbard and point it at all four directions in turn, to show his willingness to defend Church and people from all foes. Depending on the country, he would be seated on a throne (the Coronation chair in the abbey, in the case of England), presented with one or more sceptres symbolising his right to rule and obligation to dispense justice, and an orb—a globe topped by the Cross symbolising Christ's rule over the planet, which symbolised the monarch's role as deputy for Christ in temporal affairs. He would be presented with a ring, signifying his marriage to his land and people.

The bishop (or in the case of the Holy Roman Emperor when crowned King of the Romans at Aachen or Frankfurt, three bishops) would at last place the crown upon the new sovereign's head. This headgear had deep significance in each country—from the Empire's Crown of Charlemagne to the Hungarian Holy Crown of St Stephen. Either before or after this (depending again upon country and era), the king would receive Holy Communion. His wife might be crowned in a separate ceremony, after which the pair would be presented to clergy, nobility, and commoners to receive the homage and acclamations of their new subjects. Then would follow a parade of sorts back to the palace where inevitably a banquet for the country's notables would ensue. Thus, the monarch entered in his demi-priestly, judicial, and military roles endowed with legitimacy and authority from God as mediated through the Church.

This reality was reflected, in Catholic times, by the way in which the Church calendar dominated the life of the various imperial and royal courts of Europe. It was precisely because Christ at the Last Supper had merged His own Davidic kingship with the *communio* of the Church—symbolised by the washing of feet at the Last Supper—that Maundy Thursday as celebrated at every Catholic court in Europe featured the Sovereign washing the feet of the poor. This remained the case until each became liberal or was overthrown over the course of the nineteenth and twentieth centuries. Similarly with the presentation of gold, frankincense, and myrrh by the Sovereign to his Chapel Royal on the Epiphany, and (after the custom became established in the thirteenth century) his marching in the Corpus Christi procession. This would remain the case with Austria-Hungary until 1918, and Spain until 1931.

Of course, the sort of monarchy that these ceremonials graced was not the sort of "crowned republic" with which we are familiar today—even with the restored monarchy in Spain. The Church having given him authority, the monarch had sufficient power to guide the foreign and military policies of his people, all the while being obliged by his oath to respect the local liberties of his provinces and to try to coordinate, as a father would, the differing interests—clergy, nobles, gentry, guilds, cities, and peasantry—of his peoples: what we would today call subsidiarity and solidarity. All of this came to an end, of course, in different times and places, to be replaced with the sort of absolute governments under which we now live.

One of the interesting characteristics of the British nature is its ability to hold on to the shells of things long after the content has vanished. After his Coronation—so very reminiscent of that of his predecessors—King Charles III will go through the Royal Maundy every year (no more footwashing, but there is a church service and the fortunate elderly poor chosen for it receive specially minted money and a banquet)[4] and have the three gifts of the Magi presented, upon the Feast of the Epiphany, to the Chapel Royal. His springtime sojourn at Windsor will still be called "Easter Court," and, as he did this year, he will make

---

4   The custom of distributing alms to the poor on Maundy Thursday is a part of the Catholic ceremony for Maundy Thursday in the pre-1955 Missal. The coins used by the British monarch are called "Maundy money."

Christmas broadcasts emphasizing that it is the feast of Jesus Christ's birth. In short, in so many ways the appearance of what was once a Catholic monarchy will be preserved, even though the Parliament which has controlled the British monarchy since 1688 produces, in the name of freedom, governments as evil and practically atheistic as any in the world (for all that there are honourable exceptions among its members).

It would be tempting to dismiss all of this as publicly-funded LARPing (although in reality the monarchy—thanks to the Crown Estate—brings the taxpayer millions in revenue annually). But apart from the fact that the bare bones of what was once a Catholic monarchy can be instructive as to what governance could and might be, there is always the hope that somehow, someway, these bones might one day live again.

The King was anointed with real chrism. His taking the name Charles III (rather than George VII, as was thought would be the case) reminds one of the first three to bear that name: Charles I, who negotiated with Rome for reunion, murdered by Cromwell and the Puritan revolutionaries; Charles II, who came into the Church on his deathbed; and the "real" Charles III, Bonnie Prince Charlie, who risked all for his peoples in the 1745 Jacobite uprising.

Let us therefore pray for his conversion (even if it be deathbed, as with his namesake Charles II and Edward VII), and that of his peoples around the globe. And let us pray also for our own nations and their rulers, that through their conversion, something resembling old Christendom might return to this troubled Church and world.

8

The Vocation of Queen Elizabeth II and the Coronation Liturgy

PETER DAY-MILNE

WHEN THE QUEEN DIED LAST SEPTEM-
ber, the world mourned. The President of the United
States, a nation created by revolt against the British
crown, called the Queen "a steadying presence and a source of
comfort and pride for generations of Britons . . . a stateswoman
of unmatched dignity and constancy," and he ordered flags to
fly at half-mast on federal buildings for ten days. The President
of France, leader of a political elite that defines itself by the
Revolution, called her late Majesty the "Queen of hearts," and
many French mayors obeyed his order to fly their flags at half-
mast. Even Vladimir Putin and Volodymyr Zelensky were of one
mind in praising the Queen.

This chorus of republican praise was remarkable, but perhaps
even more remarkable was the atmosphere in Britain. We mourned,
and we knew that we had our mourning in common. We knew that
we had lost an exemplar of service, and our shared awareness of
our shared sentiment reminded us that we do sometimes think and
feel as one people, having attitudes and values in common. One felt
oneself using the same language as one's fellow subjects—"dutiful,"
"faithful," "steadfast." The words united us. In death, the Queen
brought us together in admiration of her, and we suddenly realised
how great a unifying force she had been in life, too.

Throughout the West, Britain's and the world's love of the
Queen has given new momentum to the monarchist movement, a
movement that is closely associated with Catholic traditionalism,
not only in France but also in other European countries, and

74

which even finds support amongst traditionalist communities in the United States, with many American traditionalists' websites featuring pictures of holy monarchs such as the recently beatified Karl of Austria. Hence the Queen's passing invites all of us orthodox Catholics to consider two questions. First, how did this Queen become so loved, and so unifying? Second, what does her life and death tell us about the role that monarchy could and should play in a renewed Europe?

In part one of this essay, I will address the first question. My answer to it will then put me in a position to answer the second question in part two.

1. The Queen and the British Constitution: "I serve"

The Queen was loved by people and peoples throughout the world, including many who had no affection for the system of monarchy in the abstract. Hence if one wants to know how she became so loved and so unifying, one will have to consider her character and virtues, which distinguished her from other sovereigns. This I shall do. But the Queen's success, I will argue, was also due to Britain's ancient Constitution, which assigned to her the very duties in which she excelled, laying out before her an ideal of Christian servant-monarchy upon which she built her virtuous life. By realizing this Christian ideal, she, in turn, brought new life to the Constitution, continuing a process of constitutional and spiritual renewal begun by her grandfather before her. The Constitution, as we shall see, was like a weather-beaten mediæval beacon, its light dulled and its frame distorted; and the Queen, building on the legacy of her parents and grandparents, was the flame with the virtue to make it take light again, and shine out bright across the world. The story of the Queen's reign is a story of the symbiosis of three generations of sovereigns, George V, George VI, and Elizabeth, with a mediæval constitutional ideal.

I want first to turn to the famous pledge of service that the young Princess Elizabeth made in 1947, at the age of twenty-one—a pledge that defined her life. Part of it is well known, but here I present a more extended quotation of it than is usual. The pledge, as we shall see, not only reveals her character, but also pithily captures the Constitution's ideal of monarchy.

75

There is a motto which has been borne by many of my
ancestors—a noble motto, "I serve." Those words were
an inspiration to many bygone heirs to the Throne when
they made their knightly dedication as they came to
manhood. I cannot do quite as they did.

But through the inventions of science I can do what
was not possible for any of them. I can make my solemn
act of dedication with a whole Empire listening. I should
like to make that dedication now. It is very simple.

I declare before you all that my whole life whether it
be long or short shall be devoted to your service and the
service of our great imperial family to which we all belong.

But I shall not have strength to carry out this resolution
alone unless you join in it with me, as I now invite you
to do: I know that your support will be unfailingly given.
God help me to make good my vow, and God bless all
of you who are willing to share in it.[1]

Before considering how these words relate to the constitutional
ideal of monarchy, we can first observe that they reveal the extraordinary spiritual maturity of the twenty-one-year-old princess. First,
note her complete embrace of the life to which God had called
her. For us today, who remember the Queen as a beloved and
accomplished ruler, it is easy to forget just how daunting a vocation
hers was. Speaking just four months before the partition of India,
the young Princess Elizabeth already knew that she was called to
rule a waning empire. The mother country itself was all but bank-
rupt, and (to take one example of Britain's desperate condition)
meat rationing was to remain in force for the first twenty-eight
months of her reign. Furthermore, when she made her speech in
1947, and for decades to come, all life was to be lived under the
ghostly shadow of the mushroom cloud. Elizabeth knew too that
she would have to rule under constant scrutiny, privileged but in
practice the tool of the government. Worse still, she would have
to rule as a woman in a world of male leaders.

Yet at the age of twenty-one, the young princess embraced
this vocation. She would not covet the nature and powers of
men, but would rule as a woman: "I cannot do quite as they
did." She would not despair at the decline of British power, but

---

1 "A speech by the Queen on her 21st Birthday, 1947," The Official Website
of the British Royal Family, www.royal.uk/21st-birthday-speech-21-april-1947.

would take the opportunities of her time, exploiting technology, as she said, to speak with a whole empire present. She would not shirk from or resent her duty, but would devote her whole life to the service of our one "family."

I talk of "duty": a queen's duty is to attend certain events, perform certain tasks, and to meet certain people with good grace. In her speech, though, there was already something more than duty. Princess Elizabeth made a pledge to serve like a knight of old, and her words were not idly spoken. For as Elizabeth knew, knights were expected not merely to perform certain tasks, but to do so prayerfully and charitably, seeking to grow in natural and supernatural virtues. The knight's commitment was not just to duty, but to duty raised up by the grace of Christian charity: in other words, to the peculiarly Christian vision of loving-service. Elizabeth was vowing the same Christian loving-service to her subjects.

Duty and loving-service were Princess Elizabeth's vows. Turning now from her declaration to her reign, we can briefly observe what is well known: that she fulfilled them magnificently. As queen, she did indeed do her duty, year after year, decade after decade, without complaint: at the parade ground and at the village hall, at dinners with old enemies and friends alike, at home and far abroad. She served for life in accordance with her oath, never retiring, never abandoning us when she was needed.

She had also chosen to love, and this she did too. Day after day, week after week, she made the fiftieth dignitary feel welcome, and she smiled kindly at the hundredth handshake. Through hard work and persistence, she formed a habit of charity, and so came to make charity look easy. Hence arose her famous smile, and the evident unfeigned happiness-in-service that so endeared her to the world. Through the moral authority that she won by her loving dutifulness and her dutiful love, she was able to build a Commonwealth family from the fallen empire, and to be a rock of stability in a rapidly changing world, becoming a much loved and much admired ruler.

The Queen succeeded through her Christian loving-service: in other words, through her virtue of charity. But what inspired the Queen to make her brilliantly successful pledge of loving-service? And what gave her the inner strength to keep it, persisting in charity amidst circumstances that would have led many other people to haughtiness, despair, or both? To answer these questions we must turn first to the Christian example and Christian formation given to her by her family, and then to the British Constitution itself.

"The King will never leave"

The Queen was formed for Christian service by her grandparents. Her paternal ones, George V (1866–1936; reigned from 1910) and Queen Mary (Mary of Teck, 1867–1953; married 1893), were perhaps the first seriously pious reigning British couple for centuries and were deeply devoted to each other. George V himself—hardworking, chaste, a nightly Bible-reader—soon become well loved for his dutifulness, much to his own astonishment. ("I cannot understand it, after all I am only a very ordinary sort of fellow," as he said when seeing the crowd's adulation at the celebrations of his Silver Jubilee.) George can be credited with reviving the idea, dormant since before the Reformation, that the Christian trappings of the British monarchy could be more than a façade, and that a king could and should be virtuous. For example, he became the first monarch in centuries to distribute the Royal Maundy in person on Holy Thursday, and thus restored an important symbol of the Christian service owed by a king to his people. Sixty years after government-ordered days of penance and prayer in the Established Churches of England and Scotland had finally fallen into desuetude, George also became the face of new interdenominational National Days of Prayer, which were called frequently during and after the First World War, and in which Catholics and dissenters were invited to participate. Catholics will remember with gratitude, too, that he insisted that the virulently anti-Catholic phrases be removed from the Coronation Oath before he would take it, and so prompted parliament to pass the repeal of them that it had first seriously considered nine years previously: for George was too magnanimous, and too conscious of his duty to all his subjects, to offend a group of them needlessly. His was an ethos of Christian service, which he held in common with his devoted queen.

As early as 1929, George was predicting that his dear "Lilibet" would accede to the throne, and later he even expressed the explicit hope that his reckless son Edward would have no children, leaving the way clear for Elizabeth to become queen.

78

He and Queen Mary helped prepare the young princess for a devout Christian reign. Notably, Queen Mary oversaw Elizabeth's strict early education, and schooled her in humility: when the fidgeting eight-year-old princess declined to go home early from a concert on the grounds that people would be waiting to see her afterwards, Queen Mary immediately sent her home in a taxi.[2]

In the next generation, George VI (1895–1952; reigned from 1936) and his consort, Queen Elizabeth (Elizabeth Bowes-Lyon, known as the Queen Mother in her widowhood: 1900–2002, married 1923), continued the spiritual renewal of the British monarchy, giving the Queen a close example of loving-service. Unexpectedly acceding to their thrones less than three years before the start of World War II, amidst the scandal of Edward VIII's abdication and in an age of Communism and Fascism, the King and Queen faced a daunting task. Soon they were leading a desperately unprepared Britain through the nightmares of the Blitz. But they remained strong to endure. Working in London throughout the bombing, they regularly visited their devastated fellow Londoners and consoled them. The King's and Queen's devotion is made clear by the famous reply of the Queen to her courtiers when they were urging her to leave Britain with her children in order to escape the Nazi bombs: "The children won't go without me. I won't leave the King. And the King will never leave."[3]

Throughout, Christian faith sustained them. George continued his father's policy of regularly attending public worship on important occasions, and not in state but in ordinary dress, something that previous Protestant British sovereigns had done comparatively rarely.[4] And whereas his father had merely been invited by the government to call the nation to prayer, George actually took the lead in proposing wartime Days of Prayer to the government. The sermonic character of his wartime addresses, some of the most

---

2   Robert Lacey, "When did young Elizabeth realise that one day she would become Queen?," *BBC News* website, 6 February 2022, www.bbc.co.uk/news/uk-60201088.

3   "The Life and Work of Queen Elizabeth the Queen Mother," The Official Website of the British Royal Family, www.royal.uk/life-and-work-queen-elizabeth-queen-mother.

4   P. Williamson, "National Days of Prayer: The Churches, the State and Public Worship in Britain, 1899–1957," *The English Historical Review* 128, no. 531 (2013): 323–66, at 344.

important of which were delivered on these Days of Prayer, was remarked upon at the time. Here is an excerpt from his speech to the nation on D-Day:

> We shall ask not that God may do our will, but that we may be enabled to do the will of God: and we dare to believe that God has used our Nation and Empire as an instrument for fulfilling his high purpose.
>
> I hope that throughout the present crisis of the liberation of Europe there may be offered up earnest, continuous and widespread prayer. We who remain in this land can most effectively enter into the sufferings of subjugated Europe by prayer, whereby we can fortify the determination of our sailors, soldiers and airmen who go forth to set the captives free.[5]

It is hard to imagine such words in the mouth of Edward VII, a Hanoverian, or even Queen Victoria. But coming from George VI, they rang true. The Queen was the heiress to a king whose public Christian witness, running against the Whig's grain of history and all expectations, had brought altar and throne closer together than at perhaps any time since the Reformation.

"Be thy Head anointed with Holy Oil"

The marriages of George V and Mary, and George VI and Elizabeth—not to mention here the late Queen's pious and loving maternal grandparents—provided the setting in which she, as Princess Elizabeth, was to grow to maturity. Her family nurtured the virtues and natural talents of the young princess, of whom Churchill had written in 1928, when she was only two, "she has an air of authority and reflectiveness, astonishing in an infant." Yet if we seek what inspired Queen Elizabeth to live her virtuous life of loving-service, then we must dig a little deeper still. For although the Queen's royal relations set her an example of Christian monarchical loving-service, they had not chosen or defined that form of service for themselves. On the contrary, in their good Christian lives they were but following, and renewing, an ancient ideal of Christian monarchy that is written into the British Constitution. This constitutional ideal was and is

---

5 "King George VI's speech on D-Day," The Official Website of the British Royal Family, 5 June 2019, www.royal.uk/king-george-vis-speech-d-day.

expressed most clearly in the British coronation rite—a rite that the eleven-year-old Princess Elizabeth had seen performed for her father and mother in 1937, ten years before her famous birthday speech.

The serious, thoughtful young girl had not failed to understand the meaning of the ceremony. During it, the choir had sung the solemn anthem "Zadok the priest and Nathan the prophet anointed Solomon king," and then the archbishop of Canterbury had anointed her parents, saying first to the King: "Be thy Head anointed with Holy Oil, as kings, priests and prophets were anointed," and later to the Queen: "Let the anointing with this Oil increase your honour, and the grace of God's Holy Spirit establish you, for ever and ever." The Church—or at any rate its woollier Anglican simulacrum—had thus confirmed and blessed the new king's and queen's power, setting them apart for the task of ruling. In the Middle Ages, the anointing of a sovereign had been understood as a sacramental, and although this understanding had been lost at the Reformation, the sacredness of the ceremony had still been evident in 1937, just as it was to be in 1953 and 2023.

Later in the coronation service, the archbishop had placed a ring upon the fourth finger of the right hand of each of Princess Elizabeth's parents—the finger upon which mediæval English spouses used to wear their wedding rings, just as bishops and nuns still wear theirs—and he had spoken mediæval prayers. The Catholics who had devised the coronation rite had seen it as effecting a quasi-sacramental, ideally lifelong bond of love, service, and fidelity between monarch and people, and the modern rite that Princess Elizabeth witnessed had expressed the same idea.

The coronation ceremony of her parents had thus taught the young princess of the quasi-marital bond between monarch and people, and of the sacredness of a monarch's role. It set before her the template for a distinctive kind of holy life: the life of the holy sovereign, bound to the service of his or her people, but also sacred and set apart.

Skipping forward again ten years to Princess Elizabeth's speech of 1947, we can see that she has by now thoroughly understood this template. Reaching back into the Middle Ages, she talks of "knightly service" and "solemn dedication," deftly expressing the status of the Christian monarch who, like a knight, is set apart for a special role by the blessing of the Church; a role of Christian loving-service. The twenty-one-year-old Elizabeth, having learnt from the coronation rites and the example of her parents and grandparents, is here committing herself to live out that constitutional ideal of monarchy.

Five years later, at the beginning of her own reign, the Queen herself underwent the rites of anointing and ring-giving. Having understood their significance so well at the age of twenty-one, as Queen she lived out the ideals that they expressed. She accepted the quasi-marital bond of monarchy and allowed it to define her, basing her life on loving-service towards her subjects. Equally, she knew that she was not only bound to her people, but also set apart from them, and in public she retained a certain detachment, never showing us too much of her private feelings except where those reflected the common feelings of the nation. This, too, was part of what made her loved and great: in a self-indulgent, emotive age, she was not too "touchy-feely"; she did not overshare. In both these ways she was formed by the ancient ritual of the coronation, but also brought new life to it, and to the ideal of Christian monarchy written into it.

"God help me to make good my vow, and God bless all of you who are willing to share in it"

Princess Elizabeth's remarkable birthday speech, with which we began our discussion, also shows us that she was quick to understand one further, and very important, constitutional principle. In it, she declares that she needs the support of the people of the Empire and invites them to share in her vow. Here again she conveys an aspect of the ideal of monarchy that she had seen expressed in the British coronation rite. At the beginning of the rite, the king—standing on a specially-constructed temporary platform called the theatre—shows himself to the people at each of its four corners, while the archbishop asks "All you who are come this day to do your homage and service, are you willing to do the same?" The rite conveys the principle of monarchy by popular consent.

This principle is an ancient and enduring component of the British Constitution. Though the institutions that claim to represent the popular voice have changed, monarchy in Britain remains a conversation between people and sovereign, not a monologue.

There is a sense in Britain that the people have the right to hold the monarch to his or her holy bond, to demand that he serve them as they want to be served. In the Queen's reign, we saw this most clearly after the death of Princess Diana. Immediately after her death, the Queen remained with her family at Balmoral Castle, wanting to protect the privacy of Princes William and Harry. Yet the people, stirred on by Tony Blair and the media, became restless. Popular newspapers demanded that the Queen travel to London, accusing her of heartlessness. The people wanted the Queen to lead them in grief, and it seemed that she was unwilling to do so. For a few days, one felt that the position of the monarchy was precarious: not because there was any threat of a revolution, but because the monarchy was losing the popular support that everyone agreed it needed if it was to survive.

Under this public pressure, the Queen came down to London earlier than planned, and led the people in grieving, with a walkabout and a well-judged speech that renewed the bonds of affection between people and sovereign. She did not what she wanted, but what the people wanted. For she understood that her power, though anointed and consecrated, nevertheless rested on her claim to represent and serve her people in accordance with their will. Perhaps at the time of Princess Diana's death that popular will was rash; but the Queen faithfully deferred to it.

Auctoritas et Potestas

I have been presenting the Queen's reign as a realisation of the ancient Christian ideal of servant monarchy, as expressed in the British coronation rite. Another aspect of that ideal merits consideration. For as we have seen, in the ancient rites of the British coronation the Church blesses the monarch and sets him or her aside for the task of ruling. In other words, the monarch is not automatically sacred, but becomes so through the sanction and blessing of the Church. This has an important implication. As the German historian Onno Klopp observed in 1891, the meaning and the motive of every mediæval coronation rite consists in this, that the monarch goes to the Church as to a separate authority, to crave her approval.[6] In doing so the monarch is reminded that

---

6 Herbert Thurston SJ, *The Coronation Ceremonial: Its True History and Meaning*, 2nd ed. (London: Catholic Truth Society, 1911), 1.

his power is limited to the temporal sphere, and that he has no authority to teach or enforce any forms of faith or morals except those of the Church. The rite also reminds him and his people that he remains subject to the moral law, with the Church having the authority to rebuke him if he breaks it. The rite thus embodies Pope Gelasius's doctrine that there is a spiritual *auctoritas* and a temporal *potestas*, both of God, neither absolute—a doctrine that defined the politics of mediæval Christendom, even as its exact meaning was strenuously contested.

In Britain, this notion of the Church's separate authority of course became weaker after the Reformation, and many mediæval coronation prayers were revised to water-down the conspicuous Gelasianism of the old ceremony. Nevertheless, the old notion of the Church's independent spiritual authority has always remained implicit in the post-Reformation British coronation rite. The archbishop of Canterbury does not consent to anoint the sovereign until he has made him or her promise to "cause Law and Justice, in Mercy, to be executed in all your Judgements," and to protect the Church of England. Symbolically, the monarch still has to satisfy the archbishop before he favours him or her with anointing.

At her own coronation the Queen made that same promise, and she kept it throughout her reign. She understood that her power, though sacred, was limited. She did not tell her people how to live or what to believe. She knew that she was subject to the moral law, and she sought to be virtuous. She also respected the hierarchy of the Anglican Communion, never interfering in its internal doctrinal disputes. She was faithful in the way proper to an ordinary laywoman and was herself respected for her quiet unimposing stewardship of the Church of England. In this way, too, she brought the British Constitution's mediæval ideal of monarchy to life.

A Chriſtian queen

I have now identified several connected ideals expressed within the British coronation rite. Together, they form a distinctive vision of Christian monarchy. According to this vision, the monarch has a holy status and an anointed power, yet this power is to be exercised under the form of Christian service, by the consent of the people. Furthermore, it is a limited power—the monarch

84

has no authority to teach novel faith and morals, and remains subject to the Church's rebuke if he strays from hers.

In her life, the Queen realised this vision. She lived a life of loving-service, as if a spouse to her people. She carried herself with the dignity proper to an anointed sovereign. She heeded popular sentiment. She obeyed her church. In doing these things, she followed the constitution's template for the life of a holy monarch, allowing it to shape and form her. Thus she grew in virtue and became much loved and admired. The secret of the Queen's success was the combination of her natural gifts, the Christian formation that her family gave her, and the British constitution, which laid before her the path of Christian service that she was to tread.

2. The restoration of the Christian ideal of monarchy

So much on the Queen herself. But what can her life tell us about the future role that monarchy could and should play in a renewed Christendom?

First, we need to broaden our perspective. As we have seen, the ideal of monarchy that the Queen lived out forms part of Britain's constitution. So far, I have discussed that ideal as if it were peculiarly British; and this has been natural enough, because today Britain is the only country in which it survives as a continuous constitutional tradition from the Middle Ages. But now we must realize that, by origin, the ideal that is still expressed in the British coronation rites was not peculiarly British at all. On the contrary, it was once the shared ideal of all Europe.

By an accident of the history of scholarship, this truth is too little appreciated. Serious English-language study of the British coronation was revived, after a long dormancy, in the years before the coronation of Edward VII (1841–1910) in 1902, which was the first British coronation for sixty-four years. But the field of research was monopolised by Anglo-Catholics, especially those of the Henry Bradshaw Society, who were always keen to emphasise the "English genius" of the coronation, ignoring the fact that many of the texts and ceremonies of the British coronation rite are similar or identical to continental ones of the early and high Middle Ages, such as those for the coronation of a Holy Roman Emperor.

There is another reason why we forget that the ideal of monarchy expressed in the British coronation rite was once the ideal of all Europe. This is simple: the ideal has survived nowhere else. In France, for example, several circumstances encouraged an excessive deference to the king. Already in the fifteenth century, one prominent French commentator, Georges Chastellain, felt able to liken the coronation entrance procession of Louis XI (1423–1483; reigned from 1461) to the birth of Christ.[7] Legends grew around the "Holy Ampule" used for anointing the monarch, and the rite was sometimes depicted as a sacrament, not a mere sacramental. A too high view of the king's sacrality slowly destabilised the mediæval synthesis of Church and state, until French kings had the power to introduce such openly anti-Christian innovations as the *maîtresse-en-titre*. Meanwhile, in Scotland and other reformed countries, the loss of any agreed-upon conception of the Church and her authority fostered the supposedly Bible-based absolutism of James VI (1566–1625; reigned in Scotland from 1567), a doctrine that he brought south when he acceded to the English throne as King James I in 1603.

These ideas, together with economic and social changes, ultimately led people to abandon the mediæval model of monarchy, and to accept monarchs like Charles I (1600–1649; reigned from 1625) and Louis XIV (1638–1715; reigned from 1643), whose style of reign upset the delicate balance of powers, the king's, the Church's, and the people's, which the mediæval model had been designed to sustain. These new, modern monarchs claimed an unconditional sacrality, and also an absolute jurisdiction over their subjects. They forgot that their predecessors' sacred status had always been conditional upon the approval and blessing of an independent, authoritative Church. They forgot too that the Christian monarch's rule, according to the mediæval model of monarchy, was to be a rule of quasi-spousal service, by the consent of the people, and limited to the temporal sphere.

Yet the new, unbalanced model of monarchy soon proved untenable. Everywhere it was tried, it soon prompted a republican, or at least a desacralising, reaction.

---

7 János M. Bak, ed., *Coronations: Mediæval and Early Modern Monarchic Ritual* (Berkeley/Los Angeles: University of California Press, 1990), 113.

The histories of Denmark and Russia clearly illustrate this process. Before the Reformation, the Danish coronation was similar in tone to England's, and during it (as in England at the time) the king prostrated himself at the altar. In 1537, at the first Lutheran-run coronation, the prostrations were omitted: already the king's servanthood and limitations were less clearly expressed now that he was commanding a blessing from his own Church. From 1660 the Danish monarchy, which had thitherto been elective, became hereditary, and explicitly absolute. As the *Kongeloven* (King's law) of 1665 was to decree:

> The absolute hereditary king of Denmark and Norway shall hereafter be, and by all subjects be held and honoured as, the greatest and highest head on earth, above all human laws and knowing no other head or judge above him, either in spiritual or secular matters, except God alone.[8]

From 1660 there was no coronation ceremony. Instead, each new king placed the Danish crown upon his own head as soon as he acceded to the throne. He then later went to his cathedral already clothed in his full regalia, the crown on his head, the sceptre and orb in his hands, and asked of the clergy not crowning, but merely anointing.[9] The symbolism was clear: the king no longer went to the Church, as to a separate power, to seek the confirmation of his rule; he merely condescended to be blessed by her.

Freed from the authority of the Church, the Danish monarchy, like most absolute monarchies, soon developed a strong tradition of disgraceful behaviour. Of the eight Danish monarchs who reigned in the era of absolutism begun in 1660, one was a pietist, but seven kept more or less official mistresses, accumulating four divorces and a bigamous marriage between them. What's more, their doing so was not seen by their courtiers as diminishing their royal authority. The idea of a virtuous or holy king, faithful to his sacred oaths, seemed by now like an absurd anachronism.

---

8 Ernst Ekman, "The Danish Royal Law of 1665," *The Journal of Modern History* 29, no. 2 (1957): 102–7, at 106.

9 Erich Hoffman, "Die Krönung Christus III von Dänemark am 12 August 1537: Die Erste Protestantische Köningskrönung in Europa," 66, in Heinz Duchhardt, ed., *Herrscherweihe und Königskrönung im Frühneuzeitlichen Europa* (Wiesbaden: Steiner, 1983).

Meanwhile, a parallel story was unfolding in the East. Peter the Great (1672–1725; reigned from 1682), one generation younger than Louis XIV, was a keen student of the latest French and Western ideas, and built up the Russian state in accordance with them. Imitating fashionable Western forms of monarchy, he exploited the latent Cæsaropapism of Eastern Orthodox ecclesiology, and brought the Russian Orthodox Church under his heel in 1721 with the creation of the Most Holy Governing Synod of the Russian Orthodox Church, a body chaired by a lay government official.

In this essay I have treated Britain's coronation rites as constitutionally significant, and it is therefore interesting to note that Russia's rank new Cæsaropapism was soon reflected in the Russian coronation rites. Until the coronation of the Empress regnant Elizabeth in 1742, the Russian patriarch crowned the sovereign, doing so with a rite which, like all Western coronation rites, was descended from the rites for a Byzantine emperor. But in 1742 Elizabeth had the patriarch bring the crown to her; she took it from his hands and crowned herself.[10] All future tsars and tsarinas regnant were to do the same. The message was clear: the patriarch was merely the altar boy of the ruler, the Church his plaything. The rite thus confirmed and advertised the Russian Church's scandalous subjection to the state.

The self-indulgent system of modern, untempered monarchy could not last for ever. In both East and West, the heady accumulation of anointed self-crowning power in the person of the king ultimately proved intolerable. The reaction in Russia was notorious: revolution, and soon Communism. In the West, the reaction happened earlier, and was the more subtle for it—but no less important. To continue the story of Danish monarchy, for example, in 1849 the Constitutional Assembly of Denmark approved a new constitution, which removed all religious ceremonial from the rites of kingly accession. One hundred and eighty-nine years of untempered monarchism had made the very notion of sacred power offensive. Ever since, new Danish monarchs have been proclaimed in an entirely desacralised way.

---

10 Brenda Meehan-Waters, "Catherine the Great and the Problem of Female Rule," *The Russian Review*, vol. 34, no. 3 (July 1975): 293–307, at 305. Elizabeth's action was perhaps suggested by the ancient Byzantine practice whereby the emperor would crown his empress consort.

The Danish and Russian patterns were echoed throughout Europe. Monarchs who held an unconditional sacred status, and who were answerable to no human authority, proved intolerable. In response, European nations either instituted new, secular rulers, or stripped their existing rulers of their sacred status. Ever since, hard power has remained desacralised throughout Europe and the West. Today, heads of state such as Joseph Biden (born 1942; President from 2021) and Emmanuel Macron (born 1977; President from 2017) are bound by no sacral bonds, but only by secular oaths. (In the United States, it is only by convention that the president places his hand on a Bible to take his oath.)

Yet if the executive powers of the West have long disclaimed sacrality, nevertheless they have retained one element of modern, untempered monarchism, namely the claim to sole and absolute jurisdiction over their citizens. Western governments, one might say, are today desacralised absolute oligarchies. Indeed, their power is all the greater for the fact that they have democratic mandates and are therefore able to get away with outraging public sensibilities in ways that non-elected monarchs hardly could.

For much of the nineteenth and twentieth centuries, the system of desacralised absolute oligarchy was not as tyrannous as it might have been—at least not in the English-speaking countries—because the oligarchs balanced their sweeping claims of jurisdiction with a sincere (if unstable) political liberalism (of the kind expressed by J. S. Mill), allowing their citizens, insofar as was practicable, to hold and express their own moral and spiritual beliefs. But lately, the inherent dangers of desacralised absolute oligarchy have become clear. In its predecessor system, even the most hedonistic of monarchs were still anointed, nominally Christian rulers; hence in public life they had at least to pay the "compliment that vice pays to virtue" (that is, hypocrisy), and could hardly pursue openly anti-Christian public policies. But today, desacralised absolute rulers such as Joseph Biden—who have far more power over the details of citizens' everyday lives than any monarch ever did—arrogate to themselves a spiritual power to teach and even to enforce new forms of faith and morals, making it very difficult for their citizens to work for, or even interact with, the public sector if they will not subscribe to the Rainbow Religion. Moreover, to compound the problem, separate spiritual authorities no longer resist such arrogations. As if to symbolise this, Biden, a baptised Catholic, has persecuted nuns who refuse to fund artificial contraception in their healthcare schemes, thus opening himself not merely to excommunication but even to anathema—and continues to receive Communion in Washington.

What is the Catholic's answer to the modern, corrupt, increasingly tyrannical system of desacralised absolute oligarchy, emboldened by democratic mandates? Well, the reaction to the Queen's death I think points to the answer. Very few of the many people who admired her would want to revert to a system of unconditionally sacred untempered monarchy, and to be ruled by a "Sun King" like Louis XIV—a monarch who claims to be God's plenipotentiary representative within his realm, identical with the state, and above popular or ecclesial rebuke. Equally, though, few of them approve of the unabashed philistines who too easily come to power in modern, desacralised absolute regimes. Many long instead for the sacredness of monarchy alongside popular and moral accountability. Without realising it, they long for the mediæval ideal, whereby the ruler is bound to the people by bonds of Christian service, having a sacred status, but one that is conditional upon the blessing of an independent, authoritative Church, which holds him to the moral law, and thus acts as a voice for the conscience of the people. They long for the ancient Christian ideal that Queen Elizabeth, though Anglican, re-enlivened and embodied. This is why her life and reign were so attractive to so many.

If we ask, then, what role monarchy should play in a restored Europe, the answer is "a big role." But our discussion so far prompts four words of warning. First, Catholics in republics, especially traditionalists, must be careful not to regard Louis XIV-style monarchism as an authentically Catholic mode of governance: on the contrary, it was a disastrous innovation that produced a disastrous reaction. Second, Catholics must realise that successful monarchies like Britain's are products of centuries of evolution, and indeed of grace: they cannot be created overnight according to any sweeping template for constitutional renewal. Third, we must remember, too, that the mediæval monarchs of Christendom had hard power. Even the Queen, for all her virtues, could not fully realize the mediæval ideal, because she had none, and so had to watch as many travesties were committed upon her people. Hence even in Britain much would have to change before the country could be said to be a true Christian monarchy.

The fourth word of warning applies most immediately to Britain but is of more general application too. As I have tried to show, the Queen's much-admired reign belongs to the story of a trigenerational spiritual renewal of the British monarchy. But the Holy Spirit is the spirit of unity, and so any true spiritual renewal must always tend towards Catholic unity, or wither and die. The tendency to unity was visible in the lives of King George V, who refused to execrate our doctrines in his Coronation Oath, George VI, and Queen Elizabeth II—the second of whom, despite an inherited wariness of Catholics, showed us great favour, even awarding the Order of Merit to Cardinal Hume of Westminster ("my Cardinal," as she called him). Yet by the time of her death the Queen, perhaps significantly, was one of the last Anglicans left alive who had been baptised before the Anglican Communion first defected from the natural law in 1930 by embracing artificial contraception. One felt that she belonged to the last generation of Anglicans who were, as a body, morally serious. Sadly, as the Church of England departs further and further from Catholic and rational morals, it is hard to see how the next generations of Anglican monarchs can sustain the spiritual renewal of the monarchy. We can be grateful for King Charles's faith; but will a King William or a King George VII protect Christians from the growing authoritarianism of wokery, or will they embrace it? Is it certain that King William will never wear a pride flag? And what will it mean for the Christian monarchy that the British constitution presupposes, and for us Catholics, if he does? These are questions British Catholics must seriously consider in the coming years. They should also remind non-Britons that the healthy Christian family life that helps build virtuous sovereigns is now scarcely possible outside of the protecting barque of St Peter. Hence any future large-scale reversion to morally serious Christian monarchy would have to be preceded by the reconversion of Christendom.

Nevertheless, there are ways in which all of us can today work towards a future renewed Christendom of true Christian monarchies, besides the obvious way of spreading the Faith. First, we can promote the key premise of Christian monarchism: that the civil ruler's power is limited because it is purely temporal. Concretely, we can do this by supporting churches, religious communities, and legal charities that are resisting Western states' usurpation of spiritual power and their attempts to enforce public conformity to their doctrines. We can also support religious leaders when they have the courage to exercise spiritual authority over the rulers who belong to their faith: for example, Archbishop Cordileone of San Francisco, who has barred the virulently pro-abortion Nancy Pelosi from Communion. Second, we can also hold our rulers to high moral standards, remembering that those standards are higher than the ruler, and that grace is the greatest asset a ruler can have.

By doing the above we can all slowly help restore the mediæval balance of powers, and so help to move beyond the various unbalanced systems of government that have distorted the political life of Europe for five hundred years. Then, we might see a renewed Christendom, with virtuous sovereigns punishing the wicked and giving succour to the just.

9
Innovations in the Coronation Prayers of 2023

Peter Day-Milne

THE BRITISH CORONATION RITE, THOUGH modified over the centuries, remains largely mediæval in its structure, ritual actions, and ceremonies, and to a lesser extent even in its texts. The recension of the rite for King Charles III was no exception.

There were, however, many innovations in the recent coronation ceremonies and prayers; and generally the change was for the worse. Here I offer a brief critique of the changed central prayers of the rite—those of anointing, investiture, and enthroning—comparing them with those used at the last coronation of a king, that of King George VI in 1937. My criticisms will fall under five headings: a blurring of symbolism; a downplaying of sacerdotal action; an excessive servility towards the king; a loss of the connection between the king's ruling well and his achieving eternal life; and a squeamishness about evil. I make them in the hope that those who oversee the next king's coronation might revert to the traditional prayers.

A blurring of symbolism

According to the philosophy of St Thomas Aquinas, God is Being itself, and all other being is derivative of Him. The beings that we humans can perceive—plants, animals, minerals—provide material by which the intellect can build up an understanding of God as Being by analogy. In a sense, the point of all en-mattered being is to lead us to God.

Thomistic philosophy well expresses the Christian common sense of the Middle Ages, the period in which the older prayers of Britain's coronation rite were written. In that period, most people saw the natural world as symbolic; they read reality like we read the letters of a book. Those of them who became clerics or religious brought this sensibility with them to the writing of prayers: they presented the natural world as a world of symbols, pointing to higher realities. Hence their best prayers were rich with vivid, concrete symbolism.

Yet the mediævals did not only read symbolism into the natural world, and write prayers about it; they also had an instinct for making symbolic artefacts and ritual actions of their own, to give glory to God and to lead men to Him. For example, the king's Robe of State is a splendid symbol of earthly glory. His removal of it for his anointing is an even more striking symbol of the transience of such glory, and the need of all earthly powers to defer to God. Equally, the king's orb, technically a *globus crucifer*, memorably symbolises earthly domain, and its being set under the cross.

The beauty of the traditional coronation prayers, even those added or revised after the Reformation, was that they provided a crisp, lucid commentary on the very visceral, Catholicly embodied symbolism of the ancient coronation ritual. Consider, for example, the traditional prayer for the investing with the golden Royal Robe and the orb, which dates from the seventeenth century, and which was used at the coronation of George VI.

> Receive this Imperial Robe, and Orb; and the Lord your God endue you with knowledge and wisdom, with majesty and with power from on high; the Lord embrace you with his mercy on every side; the Lord clothe you with the Robe of Righteousness, and with the garments of salvation. And when you see this Orb thus set under the Cross, remember that the whole world is subject to the Power and Empire of Christ our Redeemer.

The Royal Robe is put over the king, and spread around him on all sides, literally clothing him. As this physical action is happening, the archbishop enacts and explains a new symbolism. As the robe is put over the king, he asks power to come from on high; as it is spread about him, the archbishop asks the Lord to embrace the king on all sides; and once it is settled and in place, clear now in its status as a robe, the bishop asks that it might point towards the garments of salvation. This is what I call concretely symbolic language: language that calls our attention to a very clear set of visual metaphors, doing so in a way that makes them come alive and stick in the memory.

The prayers for the investiture of the regalia were heavily revised for the recent coronation. For it was decided that non-Christian peers would bring up some of the items of regalia to King Charles—namely, those items which, in the judgement of Lambeth Palace, had "no Christian meaning or symbolism." Hence it was necessary to divide the old prayers into a larger number of new prayers, one for each item of regalia, and to strip the prayers for the (supposedly) religiously neutral items of any reference to Christ.

I will not comment on whether the use of non-Christian regalia-givers was, in itself, a good idea. But as far as the texts of the rite were concerned, the change was very much for the worse. Consider the new, separate prayers for the investiture with the robe and orb.[1]

> Receive this Robe: may the Lord clothe you with the robe of righteousness, and with the garments of salvation.
> Receive this Orb, set under the Cross, and remember always that the kingdoms of this world are become the kingdom of our God, and of his Christ.

In the first of these new prayers, the connection between the king's robe and the garments of salvation is still present, but the language does not prompt one to bring the imagery to one's mind's eye in the same tangible, concrete way as the old, richer prayers. Much of the poetry in the symbolism of the garment is lost.

Next, the second of these two new prayers is even more careless of the symbolism which the single older prayer enacted and explained. Consider first the single old prayer. It relied on a deep-rooted, intuitive connection that humans make in their thought and

---

1 These, it should be said, are similar to the already-revised prayers used at the coronation of Elizabeth II, for which talk of embracing on all sides was perhaps felt indelicate. But for the coronation of a king there was no reason not to revert to the prayers used for George VI.

their language between *subjection to authority* and *being physically beneath something.* The old prayer drew on this intuitive connection to make the physical arrangement of the *globus crucifer,* with the orb beneath the cross, a sign of the world's being subject to the authority of Christ. Indeed the old prayer actually directed our gaze and our train of thought, asking us to see how the orb is physically beneath the cross ("when you see . . . "), and mentally to link this to the world's being subject to Christ. In contrast, the new prayer makes no attempt to present the intuitive symbolism of *being beneath,* or to draw any conclusion from it. It fails to bring the rich symbolism of the *globus crucifer* to life.

To use a helpful (if perhaps unworthy) analogy, the old prayer for the investiture with the robe and orb was like a pilot's "head-up display," which put little boxes and labels on important objects in the pilot's field of vision, making their significance unmistakable; whereas the new prayers flash by in a moment. Furthermore, the greater number of the new prayers combines with their blandness to weigh down the rite of investiture, making it stodgy and slightly boring rather than inspiring and poetically enchanting. One feels that the liturgists who devised the new prayers had a vague idea of how a rich, mediæval Christian liturgy should sound, but lacked the depth of understanding to write one.

A DOWNPLAYING OF SACERDOTAL ACTION

One reason that mediævals saw the world as replete in symbols was because they were accustomed to the sacraments and sacramentals, outward signs of inward workings. They understood that through them a cleric could mediate graces. Consider the two traditional prayers that the archbishop says at the actual crowning of the king:

> O God, the Crown of the faithful: Bless we beseech thee and sanctify this thy servant *N.* our King: and as thou dost this day set a Crown of pure Gold upon his Head so enrich his Royal Heart with thine abundant grace, and crown him with all princely virtues: through the King Eternal Jesus Christ our Lord. ℟. Amen.

> God crown you with a Crown of Glory and Righteousness, that by the ministry of this our benediction, having a right faith and manifold fruit of good works, you may obtain

the Crown of an everlasting kingdom by the gift of him whose kingdom endureth for ever. ℟. Amen.

The first of these prayers is a post-Reformation creation on a mediæval template, but the second prayer is a thousand years old. As it shows, the prayers by which a cleric mediates graces often take a special form, peculiar to clerical action. It takes a moment's reflection to understand what this is. For like the phrase "I order you to do this," prayers of clerical mediation are often *speech acts*: they create the reality that they represent. But unlike non-clerical speech acts, they are in the form of an injunction.

We can see this in our example, the prayer of crowning. The action of crowning is a sacramental. As the archbishop performs the physical action of crowning (the outward sign), he enjoins God to crown the sovereign with graces (the inward working), saying "God crown you...." Thus the archbishop's imprecation to God becomes part of the action through which God uses him as a channel of grace. It ties together the inner and outer actions in a way proper to a sacramental, and thus neatly expresses the cleric's mediating role. The prayer, one might add, also functions as a memorable commentary on the symbolism of the rite.

In the recent coronation, several such imperative speech acts were removed. The above prayers, for example, were replaced with the following single prayer:

> King of kings and Lord of lords, bless, we beseech thee, this Crown, and so sanctify thy servant Charles, upon whose head this day thou dost place it for a sign of royal majesty, that he may be crowned with thy gracious favour and filled with abundant grace and all princely virtues; through him who liveth and reigneth supreme over all things, one God, world without end. Amen.

There is still an injunction here, but it is nestled in a subclause ("so sanctify...that"), tentative ("...he may..."), and passive ("...be crowned"). Amidst the verbiage, one no longer hears the close connection between outward sign and inward working,[2] and

---

2 The only good thing about this prayer is that it is the first coronation prayer since the Reformation that has the praying parson bless an item of regalia rather than its wearer. One wonders whether this new Anglican blessing is due to Catholic sympathies on the part of the prayer-writer,

so one is not put in mind of the priest's mediating role. Much the same could be said of the newly revised prayer of anointing, amongst others.

The above example also illustrates another way in which the writers of the modern prayers have spoiled the symbolism of the coronation rite. Like bad novelists, the new liturgists tell rather than show. Eleven times they announce that something is a "ensign," "sign" or "symbol," but without helping us to picture the symbolism that they baldly assert. In contrast, the old rites show rather than tell. Only twice do they call something an "ensign," and never do they call anything "sign" or "symbol"; but they help us to see the symbolisms of the rite clearly.

One hopes for a restoration of the traditional, openly mediatory, richly symbolic prayers at the next coronation.

AN EXCESSIVE SERVILITY TOWARDS THE KING

As I have said elsewhere, the essence of any mediæval coronation rite is that the king goes to the Church as to a separate authority, to seek her blessing and approval, which she offers in the name of God and on behalf of the people. At the coronation the king gains his sacred status through the mediation of the clergy.

The traditional prayer of enthroning, much of which was mediæval, well expressed this subtle interplay of spiritual authority and temporal power. It ran as follows. The part in square brackets was deleted at the coronation of Elizabeth II.

> Stand firm, and hold fast from henceforth the seat and state of royal and imperial dignity, which is this day delivered unto you, in the Name and by the Authority of Almighty God, and by the hands of us the Bishops and servants of God, though unworthy. [And as you see us to approach nearer to God's Altar, so vouchsafe the more graciously to continue to us your Royal favour and protection.] And the Lord God Almighty, whose ministers we are, and the stewards of his mysteries, establish your Throne in righteousness, that it may stand fast for evermore. Amen.

Yet just as the revised rites minimise priestly mediation and hence

---

or to a mere indifference to the theological tenets which he or she, as a Protestant, ought to observe. Perhaps both.

priestly dignity, so they fail to convey the interplay of powers that is the essence of the coronation. At the recent coronation the above prayer became:

> Stand firm, and hold fast from henceforth this seat of royal dignity, which is yours by the authority of Almighty God. May that same God, whose throne endures for ever, establish your throne in righteousness, that it may stand fast for evermore.

Here there is no suggestion that the king needs the Church's blessing at all: his seat is no longer "delivered" to him in the name of God, but is just his. The prayer has an excessively servile tone that undermines the logic of the entire coronation rite. Does it perhaps reflect the Anglican clergy's loss of self-confidence, now that it has become evident that they are unable to offer any clear instruction to the faithful not only on essential questions of faith, but even on essential questions of morals?

A LOSS OF THE CONNECTION BETWEEN THE KING'S RULING WELL AND HIS ACHIEVING ETERNAL LIFE

In liturgical calendars and official lists of saints, the Church indicates the state of life of each listed saint. A king will be named "St X, King"; a queen, "St Y, Queen"; a pope "St X, Pope"; a widow, "St Y, Widow." The saint's state of life cannot be omitted from his or her official liturgical name. Hence any living person who is a king, and who wants to be a saint, knows that he will only ever be able to become "St X, King"; anyone living who is a pope, and who wants to be a saint, knows that he will only ever be able to become "St X, Pope." The Church's liturgical practice thus reminds us that one's state of life structures one's pursuit of salvation: to be a saint, a married man must be a good husband, and a bishop must be a good bishop. He cannot become a saint by excelling in some other role. That the Church's liturgy treats kingship and queenship as states of this kind shows that she thinks they must *define* the life of the king or queen. In the view of the Church, that is to say, there is a close connection between a king's being a good king and his becoming a saint.

The old prayers expressed this connection well, and so reminded the king that his very salvation hung on his faithful performance of his role. Consider again the prayer "God crown you...," above. Consider too this eleventh-century blessing, part of which dates from the ninth century:

> The Lord bless you and keep you: and as he hath made you King over his people, so may he prosper you in this world, and make you partake of his eternal felicity in the world to come. ℟. Amen.

The final, one-thousand-year-old phrase of the prayer of anointing also subtly expressed the same connection (my italics):

> ...and fill him, O Lord, with the Spirit of thy holy fear, now *and for ever.* ℟. Amen.

In the form of prayers used recently, the three references to eternal life just mentioned were deleted. The Archbishop of Westminster, in the ecumenical blessings, did say a prayer for the king's "happy eternity" and "immortal glory," but even this prayer failed to draw any close connection between the king's good kingship and his salvation.

The loss of this connection is regrettable, because the mention of it made the newly crowned sovereign aware of the gravity of his task of kingship, and the importance, for his own salvation, of his discharging it well. By failing to make the stakes of rulership clear to King Charles, the Anglican clergy failed in their pastoral duty to him. One senses here a connection with the aforementioned servility of the revised rites: for clergy who are too servile to their sovereigns are often afraid to tell them stark truths for the good of their souls.

Perhaps here one also sees traces of the tired, Rawlsian political liberalism of the British establishment, of which the Anglican bishops remain a part. For although the coronation even in its latest form still clearly conveys the idea that the monarch's rule is to be one of distinctively Christian loving-service, nevertheless these changes are just those that someone would make if he thought that the king's public service, in modern, multi-religious Britain, ought not to be linked too closely to his religious practice and the state of his soul. This is unfortunate, because the Queen's death itself showed us that such liberalism has had its day: people flocked as pilgrims to her coffin, honouring her holy reign, and thus acknowledging grace as a powerful and valuable force in public life, which cannot be somehow bracketed off into the sphere of the merely private.

A SQUEAMISHNESS ABOUT EVIL

As an American screenwriter surely once said, everyone likes to see the bad guys beat. Indeed the instinct is an important one: for as Chesterton observed, in this fallen world civilizations can only stand by a form of continuous knight errantry. We need leaders and citizens who will perform modern forms of knightly service, punishing the wicked and giving succour to the good. What moves leaders and citizens to such service? Well, in their tales of crime and war, screenwriters surely have one thing right. The "good guys" are moved by concrete examples of evil in the world—a murder, a theft, a bribe, a vicious annexation. The principle indeed is a general human one. None but the most quixotic of us are moved to take up a quest by the abstract concept of justice. No: we fight to right wrongs and defeat bad men.

It follows that any rites or rituals that enjoin us to pursue justice will be most stirring and effective if they remind us of concrete instances of evil in the world. The old, basically mediæval prayer for the investiture with the sword did so:

> Hear our prayers, O Lord, we beseech thee, and so direct and support thy servant King George, who is now to be girt with this Sword, that he may not bear it in vain; but may use it as the minister of God for the terror and punishment of evil-doers, and for the protection and encouragement of those that do well, through Jesus Christ our Lord. ℟. Amen.
> Receive this Kingly Sword, brought now from the Altar of God, and delivered to you by the hands of us the Bishops and servants of God, though unworthy.

The revisers of the coronation prayers, however, seem to have been embarrassed to talk, concretely, about bad men. They preferred, instead, bland, bureaucratic, fudging language:

> Hear our prayers, O Lord, we beseech thee, and so direct and support thy servant King Charles, that he may not bear the Sword in vain; but may use it as the minister

of God to resist evil and defend the good, through Jesus
Christ our Lord. Amen.
  Receive this kingly Sword: may it be to you and to
  all who witness these things, a sign and symbol not of
  judgement, but of justice; not of might, but of mercy.

People who heard the old prayer of investiture knew clearly
that it was enjoining the king to punish murderers and thieves
and brigands. It is not hard to imagine an avid watcher of the
BBC listening to the new prayer and imaging that King Charles'
task is to resist cuts to the National Health Service. One talks
of the banality of evil, but coronation prayers should not make
evil seem so banal that we are not stirred to fight it.

The second part of the new prayer is just as poor. It tells us
that the king's sword is not a symbol of judgement and might,
and it implies that justice and judgement are at odds with each
other. Both claims are wrong. First, the king's sword *is* a symbol
of judgement and might. (After all, it is a sword, a weapon of
war: what else is it going to symbolise?) Second, for that very
reason it is also a symbol of justice: for justice sometimes demands
judgement and punishment. *Pace* the modern prayer, there is no
contradiction between justice and judgement.

The errors of this part of the prayer make a nonsense of the
whole rite of investiture. A few moments later, the king is invested
with the rod of equity and mercy, which symbolises the mercy
with which the king's punishing justice ought to be tempered.
Hence the rite as a whole is supposed to symbolise the Christian balancing of justice and mercy, as foreseen by the Psalmist:
"Mercy and truth are met together; righteousness and peace have
kissed each other." But if the sword is itself a symbol of mercy,
then there is no balance of justice and mercy at all; and then
mercy itself becomes a nonsense, because mercy consists in a
derogation of justice. Without justice, there can be no mercy. The
modern prayers make the rites self-defeating.

Just as talk of punishment is removed from the modern prayers,
so, one might add, is talk of victory: the prayer for, amongst
other things "victorious Fleets and Armies" found no place in
this year's coronation.

It is hard not to detect a very modern cultural cringe about
manhood in these changes: a refusal to acknowledge the role of

the manly virtues in life. One also detects in them a very modern, very Rousseauian reluctance to acknowledge the existence of wicked people; one senses the editing pen of someone who talks about "challenging behaviours" conditioned into "individuals" rather than sins committed by men and women. The Catholic, of course, will acknowledge that even the worst sinners can be saved; but he will reject the feckless modern refusal to impute moral responsibility to people; a refusal which ultimately lies behind our modern reluctance to talk of evil-doers. He will reject the depressing cringing blandness of the modern prayers.

THE OLD PRAYERS AND THE CATHOLIC LITURGICAL TRADITION

I have discussed the richness of the traditional coronation prayers, all of which either come directly from, or have been built upon, the mediæval Catholic liturgical tradition. Here one might observe that the very qualities that make these prayers so moving and memorable are also characteristic of the prayers of the ongoing Catholic liturgical tradition, especially in its more authentic, "extraordinary" form. Compare, for example, the prayer for the bestowing of the robe royal with that for the blessing of a cincture worn in honour of Our Lord, as found in the traditional *Rituale Romanum* (1964):

> God, who willed, in redeeming your servant, that your Son should be bound by impious hands, we beg you to bless this cincture; and grant that your servant, who is to wear it as a reminder of bodily mortification, may always venerate the bonds of our Lord Jesus Christ, and may acknowledge that [s]he is bound to your service; through Christ our Lord.

As we can see, the same instinct for concrete symbolism animates both the two prayers over garments. Similarly, the instinct for looking at earthly matters under the aspect of eternity, which we saw above in the coronation prayers, will be familiar to anyone who has attended a traditional principal Sunday Mass in Britain, where we pray for the king:

> Adorn him yet more with every virtue, remove all evil from his path, that with his consort and all the royal family he may come at last in grace to thee, who art the way, the truth and the life.

The ongoing Catholic tradition, like the traditional coronation prayers, also squarely faces evil: consider the traditional baptismal rebukes of the devil (e.g., "So then, foul fiend, recall the curse that decided your fate once for all"). And it need hardly be said that the ongoing tradition clearly communicates the special, mediatory role given to the clergy under the New Covenant.

Curiously, all of the problems that we have detected in the revised coronation prayer, except perhaps the problem of servility, are also found in the *forma moderna* of the Roman Rite, which has lost much concrete symbolism and many signs of sacerdotal mediation, and which has a spiritually complacent tone by comparison with the old rites, talking less of the dangers of sin and evil men and angels.[3] But perhaps this parallelism of loss is easily explained. If an ancient rite is like an old English church, its fabric repaired and tweaked in every age, of late both the coronation rite and the Roman Rite have had "wreckovators" in, who have altered the building far too radically, in accordance with the fashionable ideas of the age.

CONCLUSION

If Britain still has a Christian monarchy in 2100, then the ancient coronation prayers will still seem apposite and moving. But in the unlikely event that any of the new prayers of 2023 shall have survived that long, they will, I think, savour distinctly of very late modernity. In their tone-deafness to concrete symbolism and their downplaying of sacerdotal mediation, they embody an already outmoded materialism; in their squeamishness about evil, they embody a self-indulgent Rousseauism that is the death of order; in their attempt to unpick good rulership from salvation, they express (one suspects) the tired political liberalism of the composers. The coronation of 2023 remained moving, powerful, and deeply Christian; but let us hope that the next one will not be cloyed by the dull, deflating, and inappropriate new prayers that, even in 2023, thankfully did not spoil the fundamental beauty of the ancient rite.

---

3   See Peter Kwasniewski, "Christian Militancy in the Prayer of the Church," *OnePeterFive*, March 16, 2022.

III

RESPONDING TO
CATHOLIC
OBJECTIONS

10

The King's Friends: Loyalists in America's First Civil War

CHARLES A. COULOMBE

PERHAPS FEW CONFLICTS IN THE ENGLISH-speaking world have been more mythologised than what is usually called the American Revolution, but which might be more accurately called our first civil war—or perhaps (in light of the effects on our shores of both the Wars of the Three Kingdoms and the so-called Glorious Revolution in Britain) our second or third. Far from being the struggle for freedom from tyranny that its propagandists and subsequent secular hagiographers have made of it, the Revolution was nevertheless of key importance in the history of the Anglosphere. It was one of the series of conflicts, beginning with the Protestant Revolt and ending with our War between the States (the so-called "American Civil War"), that transformed the English-speaking world from a small Catholic Kingdom on the edge of Christendom to a mighty and secularising colossus that has ever sought, since at least 1865, to remake the world in its own constantly altering and shifting self-image—a self-image now, in our time, resolutely perverse and cruel. Not only do three other nations beside the United States owe their origins to it (Anglo-Canada, the Bahamas, and Sierra Leone), but the current utter bifurcation in British and Commonwealth Realm governance, between the ceremonial and effective sides of government, owe their origins to it as well. It is also the reason why what Europeans and Latin Americans called "Socialists," Americans called "Liberals"; why what they called "Liberals," Americans called "Conservatives"; and why what they called "Conservatives" the United States do not have—at least, not as an organised force.

It was not always thus. When the first permanent English settlement in what are now the United States was founded in 1607, archæological evidence shows that there were both Anglicans and crypto-Catholics present. The latter's presence has been revealed by crucifixes, rosary beads, pilgrimage badges, and at least one reliquary buried in various pre-1610 graves. Thirteen years later, a group of Puritans founded Plymouth Colony in present-day Massachusetts. Thus, there was carried to the New World the religious and ideological split that would in a short while thrust the British Isles into the Wars of the Three Kingdoms. By the time the King raised his standard at Nottingham in 1642, Virginia had been joined by Maryland (founded by the Catholic Lord Baltimore as a refuge for his coreligionists). New England featured a cluster of colonies: Massachusetts and Plymouth, of course, with Connecticut, Rhode Island, and New Hampshire. Predictably, New England favoured Oliver Cromwell and the Puritans, and the last battle of the Wars of the Three Kingdoms took place at Severn Creek in Maryland in 1642.

The restoration of the monarchy occurred in America as well, however; one result was the foundation of the Carolinas. Another was the conquest of the Dutch territory of New Netherland, which would be divided into New York and New Jersey (which King Charles II gave to his brother, the future King James II & VII), and eventually Pennsylvania and Delaware. Twelve of the Thirteen Colonies were thus founded under the Stuart kings, without reference to Parliament. Even the Mayflower Compact, the first governing document of Plymouth Colony, the first English colony in America, and written by the men aboard the *Mayflower*, proclaimed its signers to be "Loyal Subjects of our dread Sovereign Lord King James, by the Grace of God, of Great Britain, France, and Ireland, King, Defender of the Faith, &c," no matter how much they might cheer the deposition of his son and the takeover by their coreligionist Oliver Cromwell a scant two and a half decades later. This declaration would have unforeseen results later.

In any case, when King James II & VII succeeded his brother, King Charles II, colonial administration and its problems were definitely on his mind; although allied with the King of France, he was very much aware of the growing friction between his colonies and those of his ally to the north. One measure adopted to rationalise colonial administration was to merge New York, New Jersey, and the New England colonies into one Dominion of New England, with Sir Edmund Andros sent out to act as Governor in 1686. But two years later, when news came of the King's overthrow, the nascent Dominion was dissolved, and Sir Edmund sent back to England, where he made his peace with the new authorities. Maryland would be seized from its Catholic proprietor; it would remain a royal province until a later Lord Baltimore apostatised and received it back. Virginia and the Carolinas made their peace quickly enough.

The new king led his kingdoms into the War of the Grand Alliance—King William's War it was called in America—which was the first of a series of wars against Catholic France and Spain, culminating in a crushing defeat for both those nations in the Seven Years' War, and the passing of New France—renamed Quebec—to the British in 1763. While the Jacobite uprising agitated the home isles, in the American colonies (joined at last by Georgia—named for George II—in 1732) the ongoing struggle against the French and Spanish in Canada and Florida commanded attention. Regardless of whether it was King William and Queen Mary, Queen Anne, or one of the first three Georges, the king was a mythic figure in his American colonies—chiefly as father of his peoples, and protector against the Catholic and Indian foes to north, south, and west. In the words of Brendan McConville, "eighteenth-century America became more overtly monarchical than England itself." The average individual thought the King had more power than he actually did.

Ironically, it was under King George III, the first Hanoverian to "glory in the name of Briton," that this began to change. Of course, by his time, each of the thirteen colonies had a legislature (usually bicameral), courts, and (save for Delaware, which shared that of Pennsylvania) a governor. This last named, and his colleague in Maryland, were appointed by the proprietors of their respective colonies—the Penn Family and Lord Baltimore. The governors of Connecticut and Rhode Island were elected from their own number by the local colonial assembly. The remaining eight boasted "Royal" governors, appointed by the Board of Trade, nominally a committee of the Privy Council, but responsible to the Secretary of State for Southern Affairs until 1768, when rising tensions led the government to create a new Secretary of State for the Colonies. Under the Legislature, Judiciary, and Governor and cabinet were a network of county governments whose organisations and officers were for the most part borrowed from those of the various shires—and in most States remain intact today: sheriffs, coroners, grand juries, notaries public, militia, and all. Indeed, to this day fifty-one National Guard and State Militia units first raised under the king still survive, and the National Guard claims to be the oldest branch of the United States government, dating itself back to their formation in 1636. Each of the colonies had its own power structure with varying ethnicities depending upon their respective histories. Each also had its own oligarchy: merchants in New England, and planters in the South. These controlled each colony's assembly, and, by controlling the salaries of even the royal governors, worked constantly to erode their prerogatives. In light of future events, one ought not to be shocked to learn that the four richest men in the colonies in 1775 were George Washington, John Hancock, Philip Schuyler, and Charles Carroll of Carrollton.

King George III came to the throne with several goals which, with 20/20 hindsight, make it apparent that he was doomed to have difficulties. Although a sworn adherent of the settlement of 1688 (to which he owed his throne, after all), at his accession in 1760 the new King was keen to regain the prerogatives lost to the throne since Queen Anne's day, thanks to the preceding King George's lack of English and interest in British affairs. This would put him on a collision course with the Whig Oligarchy that had ruled the Kingdom ever after. The Whig Party were the successors of Oliver Cromwell and his Puritan "Roundhead" revolutionaries and favoured the supremacy of Parliament over the King since they controlled Parliament. By contrast, the Tory Party were the successors of the "Cavaliers" that had sided with the King against Cromwell's revolutionary republicans. King George was sympathetic to his Catholic subjects' plight; he was the first king since King James II to visit Catholic noblemen, the first since him to be popular among the Catholic Irish (as was his Lord Lieutenant, the Duke of Rutland), and he would ultimately back the first Catholic Emancipation Act in 1778. This made it easier for the King to deal with the requirement of the treaty, ending the Seven Years' War, that he treat his new French subjects in Canada "as well as his own born."

Acting upon his own wishes, King George appointed a prime minister on his own (as he was legally entitled to do), namely his political mentor, the Earl of Bute. But while Bute did successfully bring the Seven Years' War to a close, his inability to get measures through a Whig-dominated Parliament brought about his downfall, and the return to the old system. The King would then resort to building up his own majority of "King's Friends" in Parliament, a stratagem that would lead in 1770 to his being able to appoint a Prime Minister he wanted: Lord North.

Up to, and after, that happy event, however, cabinets of whatever stripe were faced with a pair of terrible realities regarding the American colonies: (1) a huge debt had been amassed defending them and defeating the French; (2) the expenses continued, both in terms of protecting them from the Indians, and funding the Royal Navy to protect the colonies from possible external attack. There was no question of getting sufficient revenue to pay off any of these expenditures. But somehow to derive a symbolic pittance from the Colonies in order to show the British taxpayer, who was actually stuck with the bill run up for the said colonies, that they were not complete losses, seemed like a very good idea.

Various attempts were made, starting with the Stamp Tax in 1765 and extending over the following decade, to come up with a stratagem that would allow for this. But the very fact that the vast majority of things taxed were primarily luxuries, used by the wealthy, antagonised many of the various colonial oligarchies. These originated the catchy slogan of "no taxation without representation"—the irony of which (seeing that the vast majority of taxes most colonists paid were to colonial legislatures for which they could not themselves vote) has been lost on most Americans from that time to this. The last attempt, the so-called tax upon tea, was perhaps the most upsetting to the New England oligarchs; the East India Company tea, being cheaper than the smuggled tea upon which so many American merchants, like the Hancocks, made their money, threatened their livelihoods. The result was the famous 1773 "Boston Tea Party," which began the pattern of mobs, raised and partly employed by the well-to-do, being used against those loyal to the government. It was, as most rebellions are, the revolt of the rich against a government favouring cheaper goods for the poor rather than allowing the rich to get richer.

The following two years saw the formation of committees of correspondence; these in turn formed colonial congresses, which then sent delegates to the Continental Congress. A shooting war began at Concord on 19 April 1775. This was a culmination of a period in which Loyalists (i.e., those loyal to the King) were systematically purged from positions in local government (especially the commands of militias). Local Loyalists were called upon to swear allegiance to a new and self-proclaimed government; those who refused were tortured, robbed, and sometimes killed. Initially, as recounted in Eric Nelson's *The Royalist Revolution,* many of the rebels attempted to justify themselves on the basis that the colonies had been founded as a partnership between King and colonists, and that Parliament was interfering in their relationship. Their argument was that King George III should rule each of his colonies directly, in partnership with the local oligarchs—or rather, with the local legislature, which came to the same thing. But the King's endorsement of the Quebec Act in 1774, which featured his protection of his Catholic subjects, was too much for many Protestant and anti-Catholic sects who saw this as compromising his role as defender of Protestantism. It would be denounced by Thomas Jefferson in the Declaration of Independence, the document unilaterally declaring America independent from Britain, and in the most Orwellian terms possible. Indeed, that document was directed against the King rather than Parliament precisely because to have attacked Parliament would mean assaulting the very body whom the Congress were trying to emulate.

This illegal usurpation of power by the American Continental Congress led directly to the formation of the Loyalists as a definite party. John Adams characterised the political makeup of the colonies at the opening of the war as being roughly one third each rebel, Loyal, and neutral. Certainly, this estimation that two thirds of the population were not in favour of independence cannot be assumed to overestimate the numbers of the Loyalists—and in fact the proportion was probably rather higher. But it is very instructive to look at just where the Loyalists came from.

The American national myth has long been that the Loyalists were the well-to-do; but in reality (unless they were officeholders whose consciences would not let them break their oaths to the King, as Washington and so many others did), the rich tended to back the Revolution. But there were always exceptions. So, for example, in the South, where the Church of England was established, Anglicans tended to be rebel, and Presbyterians loyal; in New England, where Congregationalism was established, Anglicans were usually loyal, and Congregationalists rebel. But there were exceptions to every rule, and the Congregational ministers Mather Byles of Boston and Jonathan Ashley of Deerfield, Massachusetts were outspoken American Tories (that is, Loyalists), loyal to the King. The more assimilated members of cultural minorities were, the likelier they were to be rebel: in New York, for example, those Dutch who no longer spoke their ancestral tongue; Jacob Cuyler, whose Loyalist family were exiled from Albany to Canada because of their loyalty, retained sufficient Dutch to spend the greater part of his career as an administrator in the Cape Colony. The Catholic community split, with the wealthier siding for the most part with the revolutionary Continental Congress, and the poorer with the Crown. From the latter came the Loyalist Roman Catholic Volunteers of Philadelphia and the equally Loyalist Volunteers of Ireland, who launched New York City's first St Patrick's Day parade (which parade thus has royalist, not republican, origins).

During the 1775–76 Siege of Boston, the Loyal Irish Volunteers wore white cockades to show their Stuart loyalty whilst serving King George III, their reasoning being that, as legitimists, they preferred a stable Hanoverian monarchy to an unstable and revolutionary republic, for Jacobites (like the royalists during the French, Italian, Spanish, Russian and other revolutions) only ever sought restoration of the lawful monarch and hated revolution as a species of treason and disloyalty. For the same reason, those Scots Jacobites resident in North Carolina (including Flora Mac-Donald, who had aided the escape of Bonnie Prince Charlie in 1746) and New York's Mohawk Valley were all staunch Loyalists. For that matter, the Irish parish priest of the Catholic Scots in the latter group accompanied them on their forced winter's flight to Montreal in 1776 and became their chaplain—the first Catholic chaplain in the British Army since 1685. As that flight cost the Scots settlers many of their women, children, and elderly, when they formed a part of the Royal Highland Emigrants Regiment, they returned to the valley to visit their neighbours with fire and sword. So too, residents of areas that regarded themselves as neglected by the oligarchical colonial governments—such as the Appalachians, the eastern shore of Maryland, and southern New Jersey—tended to rally to the King.

Although there were somewhere in the neighbourhood of 170 different Loyalist units raised in the thirteen colonies, and they played an important role in some of the campaigns, their struggles were ultimately in vain, as we know. Part of the reason is that they were so varied a grouping of groups, united only by opposition to the usurping rebels; in this they resembled the Jacobites back at home in Britain. The British government never thought to mobilise the Loyalists until long after the rebels had begun to purge Loyalists from their positions. But worse still was what can only be considered treason on the part of Sir William Howe, commander in chief of the British forces in the first part of the war. Three times he allowed Washington's army to escape when he had it surrounded and was in a position to end the rebellion at once. Worse still, in 1778, rather than advancing up the Hudson to meet Burgoyne at Albany—thus cutting New England off from the other colonies—he decided to conquer Philadelphia. This left Burgoyne holding the bag, so to speak. The result was the defeat at Saratoga, which brought France and eventually Spain into the War, thus ensuring Great Britain's eventual defeat. When Howe returned to London, he took his seat in Parliament with the Whigs. Facing a parliamentary committee of enquiry asking why he had essentially thrown away the war, he responded "the answer to that question is political, and I refuse to answer it," as weaselly a Whig evasion as ever there was.

Regardless of his reasons, that defeat derailed King George III's attempts at constitutional reform—to the benefit of Howe's oligarchical colleagues, and their various successors down to the present. It began the definite bifurcation of British governance into ceremonial and effective sections, which is complete today. As Eric Nelson[1] put it, when the smoke of the Revolution and the drafting of the American constitution was finished, on one side of the ocean there would be a monarchy without a king, and on the

---

1   Robert M. Beren Professor of Government at Harvard University.

other, a king without a monarchy. Beyond that, the intervention by his brother monarchs, the kings of France and Spain on the side of the rebellious American colonists, made King George III feel betrayed; moreover, it killed his interest in Catholic Emancipation.

Nevertheless, the French-Canadians, led by their redoubtable bishop, Jean-Olivier Briand, had stayed loyal to their new King and were duly rewarded for it. When Fr John Carroll, a renegade Catholic priest who had supported the American Revolution, came up with Benjamin Franklin, one of the chief American revolutionaries, to try to seduce his flock from their loyalty, the bishop excommunicated him. As a result, when he was later named a bishop by Pope Pius VI, he had to go to England to be consecrated, rather than Quebec.

For the hundred thousand or so Loyalists who were forced to leave the newly independent America in 1783, several fates awaited. Many went to what are now Ontario, New Brunswick, and the eastern townships, these later becoming the foundation of Anglo-Canada. The inheritance of these United Empire Loyalists emerged first in such local oligarchies as the first-named Province's "Family Compact." In time, it gave birth to the unique Canadian "Red Toryism," as epitomised by such as Stephen Leacock, John Farthing, Eugene Forsey, and George Grant. The Scots element gave a certain Jacobite tinge to Anglo-Canadian monarchism. Other Loyalists went to the Bahamas where they had a particular effect on the Cays off Abaco Island and the Florida Keys. Some Black Loyalists went to Sierra Leone, forming part of the foundation of that people called the Krios. Many went to England, where they were quickly assimilated. Those who did not leave—such as the families of St Elizabeth Ann Seton and her husband—lived as well as they could under the new regime. Interestingly enough, when the leadership of the Southern States attempted to emulate their grandfathers by seceding from the Union, the areas of the four oldest Confederate States that had been Loyalist tended to be Unionist. By way of contrast, the corresponding sections of the nine oldest States that remained in the Union tended to be dubbed by the offensive term "Copperhead," that is, sympathetic to the Confederate cause. In both cases, the inhabitants of those areas unconsciously emulated their own forefathers in their resistance to a "glorious cause" imposed upon them by those who in their opinion already misruled them.

The victories of France and Spain over their old enemy, England, were pyrrhic in the extreme. While King Louis XVI's reforms of government and the military allowed the French to defeat the British militarily before running out of funds (an endemic problem that had doomed the French in the preceding wars), France was still virtually bankrupted. A scant five years after the war ended, in 1783, an Icelandic volcano's ashes ruined much of the crops for two successive years and the "Great Hunger" afflicted France and much of Europe, but the French King was unable to buy grain for relief, which would not have been the case were his treasury not empty. Worse still, revolutionary ideas picked up by his officers in America had spread like a disease. Thus, when the economic crisis forced him to call the Estates General, the parliament of the French nation, in 1789, King Louis XVI found his army's abilities much impaired. As everyone knows, the French Revolution and its horrors were the ultimate result.

The same poisonous ideas infected the Spanish Army, and the elites in the Latin American Spanish viceroyalties. When the French Revolutionary forces overwhelmed the French motherland, the Latin American Wars of Independence broke out. Just as the stiff, if ultimately losing, opposition to the Revolution in France is often ignored, so too are the royalists in the Latin American conflicts—although at any given time the "Spanish" armies there were at least two-thirds native-born (and often native Indian and Black).

But perhaps the greatest damage done by the outcome of the Revolution was done to the United States themselves. As mentioned, it meant that there would not be Conservatives, in the European/ Latin American sense, as an organised body on the American political scene, but only Whigs masquerading under the name of Conservatives. It is not accidental that Edmund Burke has been a hero to what passes for American Conservatives ever since. Despite his masterful diagnosis of the French Revolution, at the time of its American protype he was well described by Samuel Johnson, the British Tory writer and inventor of the dictionary, as a "bottomless Whig." As a result, such "Conservatives" have been forced to defend both 1688 and 1776 as "Conservative Revolutions," as if such a mixture of contradictions could ever exist. This, then, was entirely different from the outlook of European Conservatives who were, by and large, monarchists and, often enough, legitimist monarchists. From this situation emerged the notion that Anglo-American Liberalism was different in kind rather than in degree from that of Europe and Latin America. With certain honourable exceptions (like the Burke fan, Russell Kirk), holders of this idea were primarily concerned with economics—free market capitalism and economic libertarianism—rather than such areas as culture and academia where the battle for minds ultimately takes place; these were relinquished by default to the Left. The bogus ideology of a "conservative liberalism," partly adopted at the Second Vatican Council in 1962–65, had disastrous results within the Catholic Church, although it appears now to be becoming untenable for many in the light of the foolish political correctness and "wokedom" that it has ended up becoming.

But for all that the United States went down that route, there certainly have been monarchist individuals within the nation, from Fitz-Greene Halleck to Seward Collins and Ralph Adams Cram. Indeed, during the Revolution a delegation from the Continental Congress sought out Bonnie Prince Charlie to offer him the Crown of America. He refused the proffered throne; one can only wonder how the war, and the future history of America, would have developed had he accepted.

11

The Place of the Monarchy in Anglophone Culture

James Bogle

FOR MANY LIVING IN COUNTRIES OF THE former British Empire and Commonwealth, the institution of the monarchy is a cultural, historical, and political treasure. This attachment to the monarchy is not, of course, a matter of fundamental Christian dogma or doctrine, and neither is it confined to Christians alone: indeed, it is remarkable for the fact that its appeal crosses the frontiers of all faiths and cultures within and without the Anglophone world.

Likewise, American Episcopalians, loyal to their own country's traditions, are proud of their nation's constitution and system of government, based, as it is, upon the English common law. Some even argue that the American political system is, in fact, a form of elective, time-limited monarchy. Indeed, at its inception, there had even been a suggestion by Vice President John Adams that the first president, George Washington, be styled "his Elective Majesty,"[1] although this idea was roundly rejected by anti-monarchists like Thomas Jefferson, Benjamin Franklin, and James Madison.

Even countries of the Commonwealth which have become republics nevertheless continue to recognize the British monarch as the Head of the Commonwealth, out of a residual historical respect for British culture, institutions, and empire—and, to a certain degree, religion—to which they were once so closely connected.[2]

---

1 James H. Huston, "John Adams' Title Campaign," *New England Quarterly* 41, no. 1 (March 1968): 30–39.
2 As of June 2022, thirty-six out of the fifty-six member states of the Commonwealth are republics.

It is fashionable in our day to mock this residual respect as culturally immature. That judgement, however, is largely rebutted by the fact that even republican members of the Commonwealth still wish to retain the link, to a greater or lesser degree. It is indicative of a deep cultural resonance which remains alive and relevant, not merely as some temporary political expedient but rather as an ancient historical, cultural, and spiritual heritage.

Moreover, monarchy has certain oft-neglected advantages. No one in the past ever attempted the fundamentalist folly of imposing absolute egalitarianism on society. Our ancestors knew that it would give rise to anarchy and chaos, not equality and justice. Simply put, if all are absolutely equal, then to whom does one apply for redress of grievances against one's neighbour's wrongdoing? If none are above us, then there is no superior to whom we can apply for such redress (whether parent, employer, judge, or other authority). This, in turn, means that redress of grievance can be settled only by majorities or force of numbers, that is, by the principle that "might is right," the very harbinger of injustice, war, strife, and anarchy. The librettist W. S. Gilbert put it more succinctly when he wrote in the libretto for the famous operetta, *The Gondoliers*: "when everyone is somebody, then no one's anybody."[3]

It was left to our age to square the circle and argue that absolute fundamentalist egalitarianism is beneficial and equates with democracy. Of course, in reality, it is neither. Democracy gives a valid and formal voice to the governed subjects of the Crown. It does not flatten all to the same level. Moreover, in the Westminster system at least, the Crown is (or should be) the final protection for democracy and its last best friend. Likewise, within a family, it is the parents who must govern. For similar reasons, monarchs are called, in law, *parens patriæ* or "parent of their country."[4] Just as the ancient Roman word for "emperor,"

---

3   Gilbert and Sullivan, *The Gondoliers* (1889), Act II (spoken by the Grand Inquisitor).

4   The concept dates, in English law, from the beginning of Christian monarchy but, in 1608, was cited in Sir Edward Coke's report of *Calvin's Case* which stated "that moral law, *honora patrem* ... doubtless doth extend to him that is *pater patriæ*," *Calvin's Case* (1572) 77 ER 377; (1608) Co Rep 1a.

that is, *Imperator*, meant "commander," the office of any leader must, like that of a responsible commander, be one of accepting responsibility, taking charge, and serving those whom one leads, sacrificing selfish desires for the greater common good. That is the ideal of Christian leadership and monarchy, the supreme example being that of Christ the King, the "servant-King" who took the fullest responsibility for His people, even for their sins and even unto death upon the Cross. This, indeed, is the theological meaning of the Crown of Thorns (as royal crown), the Reed (as royal sceptre) and the seamless garment (as royal alb), symbols of service, sacrifice, and redemptive suffering. In turn, they are consciously and symbolically reproduced in the ceremonial vesture and regalia of kings and emperors alike, such as the alb, stole, cincture, cope, sceptre, orb, and crown. For the Roman emperors, this latter was the crown of Charlemagne, worn by them for a thousand years from AD 800 until AD 1806, when Napoleon Bonaparte effectively dissolved the Holy Roman Empire, the central cynosure of Christendom, the social kingdom of Christ upon the earth.

In our time, these ancient and venerable symbols are now preserved alive only in the ceremonial vesture and regalia of the British monarch, last seen in full array at the coronation of King Charles III on 6 May 2023 and, previously, of Queen Elizabeth II in 1952. This, then, is a gift of which the British and Anglophone cultural heritage can still give testimony to the rest of the Christian world. It preserves and exemplifies the kingly aspect of the Christian vocation, one of the three roles of the baptised, that is, prophet, priest, and king.[5] The kingly role is a symbol for Christian leadership at all levels of society, paradigmatically that of a king but likewise any other leadership role. The priestly role is to sacrifice and to make sacred; the prophetic role, the highest of the three, is to teach and witness to the truth. Moreover, the British monarchy, being an explicitly and expressly Christian institution, inevitably operates as a brake upon the increasing secularisation of society.

Further, monarchy, particularly Christian monarchy, is a form of government that is centred upon a family at the apex of the

---

5 *Catechism of the Catholic Church*, 783–86.

social organism, rather than upon a group of individuals who have, by fair means or foul, managed to claw their way to the summit of political power. Monarchy has the added advantage that, unlike a republic, it is forever young since, being based upon a family, it will have new and younger members every time a royal princess gives birth to another child. This tends to give monarchy a more human quality than other forms of government. A republic does not produce children in a line of succession but only a selection of often ageing and greying politicians, of no particular background beyond the world of narrow party politics, who have merely managed to attain high office by outwitting, outlasting or outmanoeuvring (sometimes corruptly) their opponents. Higher and nobler feelings of loyalty, self-sacrifice, and duty fit naturally towards one's monarch and sovereign, as to a father or mother, but perhaps not quite so well towards a mere politician who has managed to climb the greasy pole of political ambition.

Perhaps ironically, it was an early twentieth-century Irish Catholic archbishop, Dr John Healey of Tuam, Ireland, who best described the nobility of spirit engendered by monarchy when he wrote the following:

> The character of kings is sacred; their persons are inviolable; they are the anointed of the Lord, if not with sacred oil, at least by virtue of their office. Their power is broad—based upon the will of God, and not on the shifting sands of the people's will... They will be spoken of with becoming reverence, instead of being in public estimation fitting butts for all foul tongues. It becomes a sacrilege to violate their persons, and every indignity offered to them in word or act, becomes an indignity offered to God Himself. It is this view of kingly rule that alone can keep alive, in a scoffing and licentious age, the spirit of ancient loyalty, that spirit begotten of faith, combining in itself obedience, reverence, and love for the majesty of kings which was at once a bond of social union, an incentive to noble daring, and a salt to purify the heart from its grosser tendencies, preserving it from all that is mean, selfish and contemptible.[6]

---

6 Quoted in P. J. Joyce, *John Healy* (Dublin: M. H. Gill & Son, 1931), 68–69.

As a result of the once widespread geographical and global reach of the British Empire, the British monarch is a familiar figure in all but the most remote parts of the globe. This, in turn, has given the monarchy an influence and import that the institutions of very few other small countries, the size of Britain, have. There can be little doubt that this influence partly arises because of its origin in Christianity and the Gospel.

This influence, with obvious exceptions, has mostly been for good in recent times due, not least, to the personal qualities of our previous monarch, Queen Elizabeth II, a woman almost universally admired, even, it must be said, by the enemies of monarchy. That she was a devout member of the Church of which she was the Supreme Governor is a fact known by almost everyone, not least as a result of her annual broadcast at Christmas which invariably focused first upon the Commonwealth, of which she was head, then on her family and the nation and last, but far from least, upon the Christian gospel and the person of Jesus Christ, both of which have clearly shaped her own personal life.

It is notable, if not indeed remarkable, that the British monarch is one of only a few explicitly Christian leaders in the world today who still occupies a position within a living constitution. Other once-Christian countries, like, for instance, the Republic of Ireland, have long since capitulated to the fashionable trend toward secularist republicanism based upon the false and revolutionary tenets of the French Revolution. That southern Ireland has been an entirely secular republic since it gained independence from the British Empire in 1922 was confirmed by its own Supreme Court in the case of *Corway v Independent Newspapers Ltd* [1999] IESC 5, wherein Irish Supreme Court judge, Mr Justice Barrington, ruled as follows: "26. The 1922 Constitution was a totally secular constitution."

In 1937, the then President of the Executive Council of the Irish Free State, and later *Taoiseach*, Eamon de Valera, adopted a new constitution by plebiscite which came into force on 29 December 1937. It added a few additional decorative words and clauses by way of a nod to Roman Catholicism, but it remained, in essence, a secular constitution. Moreover, most of those additions were shorn away by the Fifth Amendment to the Irish Constitution, approved by referendum on 7 December 1972 and signed into law on 5 January 1973.

The chief consequence for Ireland, therefore, of leaving the British Empire has been to exchange a Christian (albeit Protestant) constitution for a totally secular constitution which, for a supposedly Christian people, must be the last word in self-contradiction. If the Irish people disliked the British Empire because it had a Protestant Christian constitution, then they only succeeded in making matters worse by adopting an entirely secular constitution. The upshot has been, unsurprisingly, the widespread secularisation of the Irish nation. Ironically, this means that the Irish state is no longer Christian at all whereas the monarchical British state (and many Commonwealth realms) remains officially Christian.

As a result of careful and flexible constitutional development, the British monarchy has evolved in a surprisingly adaptable manner. This, in turn, has ensured its survival in an egalitarian age. Indeed, one of the chief roles, now, of the monarch is to be the last resort of protection for democracy, not only in Britain but also in countries where others act in her name.

In Australia, for instance, the Governor General still has powers, called "prerogative" or "reserve" powers, derived from the monarch but written into the Australian Constitution by the founding fathers (all themselves monarchists), to dismiss the Prime Minister and government and to dissolve the elected Parliament in order to protect Australian democracy from abuse of power by politicians.[7] That this is no mere empty symbol can be seen from the fact that this power was used in living memory, as recently as 1975, to dismiss the then Labour government of Prime Minister the Rt Hon Edward Gough Whitlam AC QC who, despite not having a sufficient majority in the elected upper house to govern, had refused to submit to an election.[8] Although the Governor General's actions were regarded by many—particularly republicans—as highly controversial and considered by some as a remnant of times past, his intention was clearly to protect democracy and to restore democratic accountability to the people. The people responded by

---

7 *The Federal Constitution of the Commonwealth of Australia* (1901) (as amended), Sections 57 and 64.

8 Sir John Kerr, the Governor General, by letter dated 11 November 1975, and served in person upon the Prime Minister at Government House, Yarralumla, Canberra, on the same day, determined his commission of office under Section 64 of the Australian Constitution.

voting out the Whitlam Labour government with one of the largest majorities in Australian electoral history.9 A stronger endorsement by the people of the importance of these vice-regal (and thus monarchical) powers could hardly be imagined.

It can reasonably be argued that the republican constitution of Germany, under the pre-Nazi Weimar Republic, enabled the Nazis to seize power in a way that would have been far more difficult under a monarchical constitution. As President Field Marshal Paul von Hindenburg was ageing and dying, Hitler, as Chancellor, grasped the opportunity to manufacture a crisis (on the strength of the *Reichstag* fire), to rush through legislation, albeit illegally and unconstitutionally, hugely to magnify his own power, to abolish democracy and to merge the offices of President and Chancellor into a new dictatorial office entitled "leader" or, more familiarly, "*Führer.*"

The process was called *Gleichschaltung* ("synchronisation"), begun before Hindenburg died and completed thereafter. It included, in 1933, the *Reichstagsbrandverordnung* (the *Reichstag* Fire Decree), the *Ermächtigungsgesetz* (the Enabling Act) and, in 1934, the *Gesetz über den Neuaufbau des Reiches* (the Law Concerning the Reconstruction of the *Reich*) and the *Gesetz über das Staatsoberhaupt des Deutschen Reiches* (the Law Concerning the Highest State Office of the German *Reich*) passed by the Cabinet on 1 August 1934 immediately before Hindenburg died, among numerous other acts. They carefully ignored Hindenburg's last wish that the Hohenzollern monarchy be restored. For want of a sovereign to prevent it, Hitler illegally seized power and became dictator. He then held a referendum to endorse his seizure of power, but the voting was widely corrupted and manipulated through intimidation, vote-rigging, and ballot-fixing by his brownshirted stormtroopers of the *Sturmabteilung* (SA for short).

If Germany had still been a monarchy, the king could have used his residual royal prerogative powers to veto any such attempted unconstitutional *coup*, dismiss the Chancellor and government and compel them to submit to the people in an election. The lack of such an impartial royal guardian or "umpire" of the Weimar Constitution opened a fracture which an evil and dictatorial genius

---

9 See "1975 Federal Election," http://australianpolitics.com/elections/federal-1975.

was able to exploit with the most far-reaching and, ultimately, devastating consequences. Hitler cleverly exploited and perverted the word "*Reich,*" meaning "Empire," "Realm" or "Commonwealth," to give Germans the impression that he was returning Germany to its roots when, in fact, he was, as a republican, permanently cutting those roots.

Unlike a presidency which, when the occupant dies in office, necessitates an inevitable, and exploitable, time lag between death and a fresh election, a monarch is immediately succeeded by his or her heir, in accordance with the hereditary principle. This, a principle that many see as anachronistic and outdated, is, in fact, a powerful and important bulwark against tyranny and a potentially vital protection for democracy. Indeed, this combination of the two principles—hereditary and democratic—may be the best constitutional safeguard for any state.

On a broader historical canvas, the history of Christianity is intimately interlinked with monarchy. It is a matter of historical record that Christianity, beginning with the birth, ministry, and death of Jesus Christ, commenced within the framework of the Roman Empire and owed its early rapid spread to the existence of that empire into which Christ was born and through which Christianity grew and came to flourish (albeit enduring numerous strong persecutions at the outset).

Ultimately, Christianity was victorious over the pagan Roman power that sought to persecute and eradicate it, so much so that even the Roman Emperor himself became Christian, beginning with Emperor Constantine I the Great. He, it is said, won a famous victory over his enemies after seeing an extraordinary vision of the *Chi-Rho* symbol—the first two letters in the Greek word for Christ, Χριστος or "Christos," and later a potent Christian symbol.[10] It is said that he also saw the words (in Greek) Εν Τούτῳ Νίκα ("*en toutōi nīka*"), rendered in Latin as "*in hoc signo vinces*" and in English as "in this sign thou shalt conquer," meaning that, under the sign of Christ he would gain the victory.[11] Constantine ordered that the

---

10 Lactantius, *Lucii Cæcilii liber ad Donatum Confessorem* from *De Mortibus Persecutorum*, in *The Works of Lactantius* II, Ante-Nicene Christian Library: Translations of the Writings of the Fathers down to AD 325 (Edinburgh: T. & T. Clark, 1867 to 1885), vol. 22, p. 203.
11 Eusebius of Cæsaria, *Vita Constantini*, AD 339 (London: Samuel Bagster and Sons, 1845), chs. 28–31.

letters of the *Chi-Rho* be painted on the shields of his troops and he then went on to win a resounding victory over his enemies at the Battle of the Milvian Bridge on 28 October AD 312. Thereafter he favoured Christianity, allowing it to spread all over the Roman Empire. This included to Britain, the country of his acclamation as *Cæsar* and Western Emperor, by the army, at *Eboracum*, now the city of York, in AD 306 after his father, also Western Emperor, had died. He was himself later baptised a Christian.

His later successor, the Emperor Theodosius I the Great, made Christianity the official state religion of the Roman Empire, replacing the old pagan Roman religion.[12] From that time, the laws of the Roman Empire were conformed to the teachings of Christ and of the Christian religion and, gradually, over time, the majority of the people of the empire became Christian, including in Romanised Britain. This, then, was the beginning of that concept once familiar to all Christians, and still familiar to Anglicanism today, that the State is officially Christian, though recognizing the freedom of its members to follow other religious traditions. In the historical context this unique arrangement was called "Christendom," or the temporal (i.e., social and political) kingdom of Christ upon the earth.

It is one of the remarkable facts of our time that, in many of the formerly Catholic countries, the idea of Christendom has gradually been eclipsed by the advent of an increasingly secularist state. In contrast, in the historically Protestant countries, like Britain, the Netherlands, and the Scandinavian countries, although secularism has advanced in many ways just as rapidly there, nevertheless the traditional idea of a Christian monarchical state has survived surprisingly well.

In Britain, Christianity first found fertile soil among the ancient *Prythani*, or "Britons," who were soon persuaded to abandon their pagan beliefs as readily as the woad that their warriors had worn as war paint when the Romans first arrived under Julius Cæsar in 55 BC. When a new wave of pagan barbarians, coming from the east, began to overrun the Roman Empire, by then still a fledgling Christian Commonwealth, the legions were compelled to withdraw from the furthest reaches of the empire, leaving behind Romano-Christianised native populations to fend for themselves.

---

12 *Edictum Gratiani, Valentiniani et Theodosii de Fide Catholica*, 27 February 380, in *Codex Theodosianus*, XVI, 1, 2 (Paris: Magnou-Nortier, 2002).

Britain was no exception and the Romanised Celts (the ancestors of the *Cymri*, or Welsh people) who remained, continued to build and defend their Christian civilisation to such an extent that legends have famously survived with later embellishments, for example the legendary tales of King Arthur and his Knights of the Round Table, all Christian Romanised Britons.

Whilst these Romanised Britons were eventually defeated militarily by invading pagan Germanic tribes from the fifth to the seventh centuries, their Christian religion eventually won over the invading Anglo-Saxons and Jutes, for it is part of the genius of Christianity that it prefers to conquer its enemies by turning them into friends.

Queen St Bertha (or St Aldeberge, c. 565–601) was the Queen of Kent whose influence led to the Christianisation of Anglo-Saxon England. She was a Frankish princess and great-granddaughter of King Clovis I, the first Christian King of the Franks, and his Queen, St Clotilde, who, in turn, had converted him.[13]

In similar fashion, in AD 580, Queen St Bertha married, and eventually converted, King St Æthelberht of Kent who, thereafter, endorsed and supported the missionary Benedictine monks, led by St Augustine of Canterbury, sent, in AD 596, by Pope St Gregory I the Great to restore Christianity to Britain.[14]

Famously, Pope Gregory had seen blonde-haired and blue-eyed pagan Anglo-Saxon children being held as prisoners in the Roman captives forum and marvelled at their appearance, likening them to little angels.[15] On being informed that they were Angles, St Gregory remarked *"non Angli sed angeli, si forent Christiani"* — "not Angles but angels, if they were Christian" — and vowed to send a mission to their country to evangelize them.[16] So began the genuinely Anglo-Saxon, later English, form of Christianity.

---

13 She was the daughter of King Charibert I and Queen Ingoberga, and granddaughter of King Chlothar I.

14 St Bede, *Historia Ecclesiastica Gentis Anglorum* (Ecclesiastical History of the English People), trans. A. M. Sellar (London: George Bell and Sons, 1907), Bk. I, ch. 25; Bk. II, ch. 5.

15 There being few prisons in those days, it was the ancient custom to reduce captive prisoners of war, and sometimes their families, to indentured servitude for a fixed term (release often taking place at the Biblical Jubilee). Christianity ensured that the captives were treated fairly and humanely. This was to be distinguished from true or "chattel" slavery and it was Christianity that eventually caused chattel slavery to be abolished altogether.

16 St Bede, *Historia Ecclesiastica Gentis Anglorum*, Book II, chapter 1.

Because, after the later Norman Conquest, so much of Anglo-Saxon culture was lost, only remnants have been bequeathed to later generations but, from what has remained, we are able to catch a glimpse of a deeply Christian society founded upon a strong monarchy.

Anglo-Saxon monarchy is also famous for its remarkable number of royal saints such as St Edmund, king and martyr, the original patron saint of England before St George, introduced from the East by crusader knights, became more popular. Others in that glorious array[17] include King St Alfred the Great (a saint by popular acclaim, rather than canonical process), Kings St Athelstan I, St Edward the Martyr, and St Edward the Confessor, and Princesses St Æthelburh of Wilton, St Frideswide of Oxford, and St Edith of Wilton and Kemsing, to name but a few.[18]

In Scotland, Christianity was introduced to the Picts and Scots during the Roman occupation of Britain. After the Anglo-Saxon invasion, paganism returned to southern Scotland but, in the sixth century, missionaries like St Ninian (Finnian), St Kentigern (Mungo) and St Columba arrived, the latter founding the monastery at Iona from where he carried out missions to the Scots of Dál Riata. Early Scots kings like Fergus the Great (*Fergus Mòr Mac Earca*), Constantine (*Causaintin*) and Angus (*Œngus*) were Christian, as was Kenneth I MacAlpin (*Cináed mac Ailpín*).

Most of Ireland had remained Christian since after the time of St Patrick, himself a Romanised Briton, its high kings emulating the other monarchs of Christendom. By this time, the centre of Christendom had moved, after the barbarian invasions, to the East, at Constantinople, the city of Constantine the Great. The ancient, flourishing culture of Byzantium and Eastern Christianity stems from this transfer. The political structure was again monarchical, with the Eastern Roman Emperor as the cynosure and central figure alongside the pope. All of Christendom, including the

---

17 Susan J. Ridyard, *The Royal Saints of Anglo-Saxon England* (Cambridge: Cambridge University Press, 1989).

18 By contrast, the number of republican presidents canonised by the Church is zero, although it is possible that Gabriel García Moreno, nineteenth-century president of Ecuador, might one day be canonised (but then, it must be said, he was a lifelong monarchist). See Mary Monica Maxwell-Scott, *Gabriel García Moreno, Regenerator of Ecuador* (London: R. & T. Washbourne, 1914).

kings of England and the high kings of Scotland and of Ireland, recognised Byzantium as the genuine Christian successor of the original Christian Roman Empire based on Rome.

However, with the decline of the Eastern Roman Empire (partly due to Islamic invasions) and threatened by a new wave of barbarian invasions, the people of Rome and the West began to fear for their very survival. Since they were unable to rely any longer upon the Eastern Roman Emperor for aid, they turned to Charlemagne, the newly powerful Christian king of the ever-growing nation of the Franks.

Famously, on Christmas Day AD 800, with the sanction and blessing of Pope St Leo III, the nobility, clergy, and freemen of the city of Rome gathered in St Peter's Basilica and elected, by acclamation, Charlemagne as the revived Roman Emperor in the West.[19] This development had a huge impact upon Western culture, not least in England, Scotland, Wales, and Ireland. Thereafter Christian kings in the West began to model themselves upon the person, cult, and court of Charlemagne. The English monarchy was no exception and it, and the high kings of Scotland and of Ireland, directly imitated the Frankish imperial court. The central position of the Christian Emperor was so clearly endorsed by the Church that, from time out of mind, until the fall of the Habsburg monarchy in 1918, the universal Church prayed expressly for the emperor, directly after the pope and clergy, in the Great Intercessions on Good Friday and in the *Exultet* on Holy Saturday at the Solemn Easter Vigil.[20] These imperial prayers, in Latin, extolling the special position of the Holy Roman Emperor, included the "Bidding" in the Good Friday Great Intercessions which may be translated thus:

---

19 Einhard, *Vita Karoli Magni*, trans. A. J. Grant (Ontario: Medieval Latin Series, 1999), 28.

20 The prayers for the emperor were no longer said after 1918, with the fall of the Austro-Hungarian Empire, but remained part of the Roman Rite until 1956, at which time a new prayer for rulers in general—*pro omnibus res publicas moderantibus*, "for those in public office"—was substituted. This prayer was changed again following the Second Vatican Council and placed right at the end of the intercessions, behind the prayers for unbelievers and atheists, signifying the complete lack of importance that a clericalist and Modernist like Archbishop Bugnini now attributed to the laity and to the lay temporal power, in stark contrast to Pope St Gelasius I in his blueprint for Christendom, *Famuli Vestræ Pietatis*, of 494.

> Let us pray also for the most Christian Emperor...that
> the Lord God may reduce to his obedience all barbarous
> nations for our perpetual peace.

The collect that follows begins thus:

> O God, who prepared the Roman Empire for the preach-
> ing of the Gospel of the eternal King...

Court ceremonial was developed, from ancient Roman rituals, under Charlemagne, partly influenced by his chief minister of education, the Anglo-Saxon Benedictine monk, Alcuin of York, venerated as a saint in both the Catholic Church and the Angli-can Communion. The imperial coronation ceremonial, once so prominent in Western Christendom, now only survives, in its full form, in the British coronation ceremonial, and therefore remains part of the wider Christian cultural heritage.

Although the imperial office, by reason of time-honoured Roman tradition, was an elective office, most other Christian monarchies (but not all) retained the hereditary principle as primary. Origi-nally, the imperial and papal electorates were the same, namely the nobility, clergy, and freemen of the city of Rome, but as the civil disorders often engendered by such forms of election became evident, the electoral privilege was deputed to colleges of electors (a concept familiar in American presidential elections).

For a pope this became the college of cardinal-princes. For an emperor it became the college of prince-electors (originally num-bering seven), each also holding ancient Roman imperial offices, reflecting their closeness to, and personal service upon, the Roman emperor. The number seven is often held, in Christian tradition, to be the number of completion—hence seven sacraments, seven deadly sins and contrary virtues, seven days of the week, seven orders of clergy, seven day hours of the Divine Office (Lauds, Prime, Terce, Sext, None, Vespers, and Compline—Matins being a night office) and so on. The original seven Prince-Electors of the Holy Roman Empire were the three principal archbishops, namely of Cologne, Mainz, and Trier (Arch-Chancellors of Italy, Germany and Gaul & Arles, i.e., Burgundy, respectively), the King of Bohemia (Imperial Arch-Cupbearer or Arch-Butler), the Duke of Saxony (Imperial Arch-Marshal), the Margrave of Brandenburg (Imperial Arch-Chamberlain) and the Count-Palatine of the Rhine (the Imperial Arch-Steward or Arch-Seneschal). The Prince-Electors, being concerned with the government of their own states, delegated by "commission" to other nobles the performance of these imperial offices, later also in a hereditary succession.

For example, the Imperial Hereditary Lord High Steward of the Holy Roman Empire, or *Reichserbtruchsess*, holding "in commission" from the Count-Palatine of the Rhine, was the Count-Imperial of Waldburg zu Zeil und Trauchburg. Palatine and imperial counts held their estates directly (or "immediately") from the emperor, palatine nobles having, historically, the closest relationship to the emperor, being successors of the paladins of Charlemagne, his closest peers. The term derives from the fact that the Roman Emperor's closest peers dwelt with him on the Palatine hill in Rome (the Roman hill traditionally thought to be the location of the cave where the founders of Rome, Romulus and Remus, are said to have been suckled as infants by a she-wolf). The English word "palace" has the same origin. The title exists in Britain, too. For example, the English counties of Durham, Cheshire, and Lancashire are all "counties palatine."

The same or similar titles were reproduced in the Great Officers of State of all the kingdoms and principalities of Christendom. England, Scotland, and Ireland were no exception but the important difference, so far as Britain is concerned, is that these Great Officers of State continue to exist (as also in Ireland until it became a republic in 1948) as part of the Christian Constitution of these kingdoms.

In England, these Great Officers of State were—and still are— the Lord High Steward (vacant now except for coronations and trials in the House of Lords), the Lord High Chancellor, the Lord High Treasurer (now usually held in commission by the Prime Minister of the day as First Lord of the Treasury and the Chancellor of the Exchequer as Second Lord of the Treasury), the Lord President of the Council, the Lord Privy Seal, the Lord Great Chamberlain (held "in gross"[21] by a number of ladies and gentlemen but currently exercised by the 7th Baron Carrington), and the Lord High

---

21 Offices of State are held "in gross" by the principal hereditary officeholders and "in commission" by delegates of the principal hereditary officeholders, chosen by the monarch on the advice of the Prime Minister or other minister.

Constable (whose function is now largely deputed to another Great Officer of State, the Earl Marshal, an ancient office not originally one of the seven Great Offices). The office of Earl Marshal is hereditarily held by the Roman Catholic dukes of Norfolk.

The office of Lord High Admiral, also not originally one of the seven Great Offices but which dates back to the fifteenth century, has been, since the eighteenth century, held in commission by the Commissioners for Exercising the Office of Lord High Admiral of Great Britain ("the Admiralty Board") headed by the First Lord of the Admiralty. When the Ministry of Defence was created in 1964, the office of Lord High Admiral was revested in the monarch, but her Majesty later conferred it upon her husband, Admiral of the Fleet the Prince Philip, Duke of Edinburgh. It is now once again held by the present monarch, King Charles III.

Scotland has similar Great Officers of State, although some were lost or forfeited after the unsuccessful Jacobite uprisings of 1715 and 1745 against the new choice of dynasty, the German Hanoverians, following the revolution of 1688.

The Jacobites, so named after King James II of England and Ireland and VII of Scotland, were those who sought to restore the Catholic Stuarts who had been unconstitutionally ousted from the throne by the revolution of 1688 for being Roman Catholics and for tolerating Catholicism and other minority religions (including Jews and Muslims), as King James II and VII had done in his Declarations of Indulgence. The Jacobites also sought to restore the ancient constitution of the kingdoms of England, Scotland, and Ireland, each as separate kingdoms, with their own parliaments, all under one Crown. These legitimist Jacobites were, however, eventually defeated by the exclusively Protestant, Hanoverian government whom Jacobites rejected as illegitimate revolutionaries.

Many under the Hanoverian regime seized the opportunity to enrich themselves at the expense of the urban and rural poor, by the slave trade and by financial chicanery in the city of London. Furthermore, the post-1688 revolutionary government imposed a savage penal code upon any who did not conform to the state religion—Anglicanism in England and Ireland and Presbyterianism in Scotland.

In an early ecumenical gesture, the Duke of Brunswick-Lüneburg (Hanover), despite being Protestant, was, in 1692, promoted to prince-electoral status within the Catholic Holy Roman Empire. This was acceptable to Catholic rulers because the Prince-Elector of Brandenburg had remained an imperial elector even after he had become a Protestant during the Reformation, as had the Prince-Elector Palatine. The Hanoverians, even after being chosen by the anti-Catholic English government to be kings of Great Britain and Ireland, remained imperial prince-electors and are referred to as such, in documents and letters, by the rebellious American Colonists.

It is a simple historical fact, however, that the anti-Catholic English Parliament, after the revolution of 1688, unconstitutionally excluded from the throne no fewer than fifty-five princes, forty-eight of whom were bypassed for the sole and only reason that they were Roman Catholics. Parliament chose, instead, the Prince-Elector of Hanover, later King George I, a Protestant. Upon arrival in England, the Parliament-appointed King George I (with a mistress on each arm, his wife remaining locked in a castle back in Hanover) was jeered at by the people. Of his two German mistresses (Frau Schulenburg, later Duchess of Kendal, and Countess von Platen, later Countess of Darlington), one reputedly thrust her head from the window of the carriage and called out in poor English, "Good people, why you wrong us? We have come for all your goods!" (meaning "good"), to which one Londoner wag in the crowd replied, "Aye, and for all our chattels, too!"[22]

King George I and his son, King George II, were unpopular with the majority of the British and Irish people: there was rioting at the coronation of King George I on 20 October 1714 in over twenty towns in England alone, and the Jacobite cause to restore the Royal Stuarts was at its height during their reigns. The following year, on 6 September 1715, the standard was raised at Braemar by the Earl of Mar, beginning the first of several attempted Stuart restorations which were supported as much by Episcopalians and many Presbyterians as by Roman Catholics.

There were originally seven Great Officers of State in England, Scotland, and Ireland, just as there had originally been seven Prince-Electors of the Holy Roman Empire. The currency of

---

22 Quoted in the review of James Hogg's "The Jacobite Relics of Scotland" in *The Scots Magazine — The Edinburgh Magazine and Literary Miscellany* VI (Edinburgh, 1820), 35.

these Great Offices is such that, even until 1948, when the Attlee government abolished the process,[23] peers were still tried in the House of Lords with the Lord High Steward, the highest Great Officer of State after the monarch, presiding over the trial. In such cases, the Lord High Chancellor, the usual presiding officer in the House of Lords,[24] was appointed temporarily to be Lord High Steward.

The last such trial was that of Edward Russell, 26th Baron de Clifford, in 1935 for motor manslaughter.[25] The case so caught the public imagination that it provided the central theme for one of the novels of Dorothy Sayers (herself a devout Anglican), entitled *Clouds of Witness*, in which the fictional Duke of Denver, brother of the eponymous aristocratic private detective, Lord Peter Wimsey, is tried for murder.

In Britain, as in the rest of Christendom, the monarchical principle remained, for most of Christian history, the central political reality of the Christian world. Even those Christian states that called themselves "republics" were, in reality, variants of monarchy, for example, the Italian maritime republics of Florence, Genoa, Siena, and Venice. Indeed, so great has been the influence of Christian monarchy that even modern republics, like that of the United States of America, retain many hallmarks that derive from the monarchical tradition, for example, the classical architecture adorning many American state buildings; the US dollar which derived from the imperial *thaler*;[26] the wide powers of the US president (originally based upon those of King George III whom the presidency replaced); and various procedures in the Congress such as, for example, trial by impeachment.

---

23 By the Criminal Justice Act 1948. The House of Lords still has the power to try by impeachment or by attainder.
24 Now replaced, since the Constitutional Reform Act 2005, by the entirely confected office of "Lord Speaker," a constitutionally illiterate title devised by the Blair government who clearly did not understand (or care about) the constitutional significance of the Great Officers of State. The Speaker is the presiding officer of the House of Commons, not the Lords, and represents the Commons to the monarch and the House of Lords. The obvious choice to be presiding officer of the Lords would have been the Lord High Steward as the most senior Great Officer of State.
25 *Hansard*, HL Deb 4 December 1935, vol. 99, cc48–9, cc145–50 et seq.
26 From New Netherland (New York), the *leeuwendaalder* or "lion dollar," deriving from the imperial *thaler*, spread to all Thirteen Colonies.

Conversely, many so-called "modernisers" today so often think that modernising must necessarily mean abolishing colour, pageantry, and tradition, replacing it with the monochrome, the dull, the oppressive and even, occasionally, the outright tyrannical. They even call this "progress" or "progressive." It is, in reality, neither.

The idea of Christendom—the social kingdom of Christ upon the earth—once so hugely important to the temporal constitution of Catholic Christendom, is now, as noted above, in some ways better preserved by Protestant monarchies than in many once-Catholic countries, many of whom have simply capitulated to secularism. Even when King Henry VIII broke with Rome, he was determined to retain all the customs and traditions of imperial Christendom and expressly regarded his own kingdom as an "empire" of its own, with himself as the new emperor. As some modern historians are now arguing, the cause of the break was not just his matrimonial disputes, but also his anger at having lost the imperial election of 1519 to Emperor Charles V, his Spanish wife's Habsburg nephew. He later determined to start an empire of his own.

Thus, by a twist of fate, monarchy continued to be seen as an essential ingredient in English Christianity, even after the Protestant Reformation. It has since become a permanent and prominent feature of the British and Anglophone heritage. Arguably, the preference for monarchy has preserved Britain, and parts of the Commonwealth, from tyranny—not least the tyrannies of Communism and Nazism. The monarchy has, indeed, become so much a part of the warp and weft of British and Commonwealth society that ancient traditions associated with the monarchy continue to this day, for example the so-called "Maundy money" is still given out by the monarch on Maundy Thursday,[27] in memory of the royal doles given out to the poor by the Christian monarchs of times past. The chivalric orders bestowed by the monarch remain deeply Christian in symbolism, for example the Order of the Garter is still given in the name of "God, our Lady and St George."

Monarchy in Britain is expressly and openly Christian and so remains an important part of the British and Commonwealth

---

27 Annually at the Royal Maundy Service.

cultural heritage. As a consequence, reverence for our Christian monarchy and monarch continues to play a role in the lives of many British and Commonwealth Catholics today. Notwithstanding contrary trends in British society, the monarchy still provides a wholesome testimony to Christian governance, a form of government that has enjoyed the favour of the Church and the Christian people for most of Christian history, time out of mind.

12

On Monarchy
and Tradition

Joseph Shaw

THE SPECTACLE IS UNDENIABLY IMPRES-
sive, though predictable and in part long-planned. Even
those whose own values do not align with the underlying
message can but stand in awe, in fact, at the scale of the thing,
and the depth of feeling it so clearly evokes.

I am referring, of course, to the reaction of the American left-
wing media to the death of Queen Elizabeth.

While the press of other countries, like their political leader-
ships, has reacted in a dignified and respectful way to this seismic
and melancholy national event, the American left-wing media,
led by the *New York Times*, gave us a display of rage and hatred
that was a bit unhinged. There are many reasons for this that
I do not intend to explore; more troubling for non-Americans
than the "woke" ravings of the Left is the fact that, as I have
discovered over the years, a degree of incomprehension and
even hostility to the institution of monarchy is not limited, in
America, to one side of the political divide. It even extends to
some traditional Catholics.

I want therefore in this chapter to take the opportunity to
try to give an explanation and defence of the British monarchy,
at least to traditionally-minded Catholics, who should be more
open-minded about it than "the gray lady" of New York. I will
do so in three stages. First, I will say something about the role
and importance of human traditions; then about the monarchy as
an institution; and finally, specifically about the British monarchy,
and Queen Elizabeth II.

HUMAN TRADITIONS

I start with human—that is, non-divine—traditions because the anti-traditional attitude is so powerful in secular culture that even some Catholics who accept the importance of divine Tradition with a capital "T," as a source of Revelation in Catholic theology, can be dismissive of any other kind of tradition. It is one thing (they might say) to acknowledge that Jesus Christ revealed things to the Apostles which were not written down in Scripture, which therefore come to us by Tradition; it is quite another to feel obliged to do (or believe) things simply because some fallible humans in the past happened to choose to do (or believe) them. And that is what human traditions are, are they not?

Well, not quite. I would define traditions as those practices which have been performed by our predecessors (ancestors, predecessors in the Faith, previous incumbents in the roles we fill, etc.), which (a) have been continued over time by successive generations (not necessarily without breaks), and (b) have been regarded as significant, and are therefore (c) regarded as binding to some degree on the present generation.

Thus, it is likely that we feel that we *ought*, in some sense, to continue various inherited cultural practices, such as Thanksgiving dinners, Christmas trees, attending Shakespeare plays, and so on. There may be reasons why it is impossible, on a particular occasion, and it may be that we were not ourselves inducted into the tradition in our own families, but if we see ourselves as members of a cultural group that is historically characterised by some practice, we can adopt or revive it.

These things have value because things *characteristic* of a cultural group are *markers of identity*. They give members of the group shared experiences and a sense of belonging, both synchronically, with other living members of the group, and diachronically, with previous generations. Discussions about the origins of the practices are usually beside the point. If members of a group identify them as things they *ought* to perform, *because* they are members of the group, they will function as markers of identity. A cultural group must, by definition, have traditions to distinguish it from other groups.

We want to be members of cultural groups because it gives us a sense of belonging. We could meet our physical needs in a bland, impersonal hotel, but what we want to live in is a *home*. Home is where we can relax and *be ourselves;* it is characterised by things that distinguish it from *other people's homes.* Some of these markers of identity will be specific to one's nuclear family, others to wider groupings of which one is also a member. These locate one in a group which may be of practical assistance (say, in a calamity), in terms of who we feel ourselves to be, and where we are located in history. They prevent us from being, in Pope John Paul II's striking phrase, "prisoners of the present."[1]

Ecclesial and political institutions include a range of cultural groups, but also have a cultural manifestation of their own. Cultural identities can be combined: one can be Irish, an American citizen, and a Catholic, culturally, all at once. If the Church or political institutions were to weaken as cultural identities, this would weaken members' sense of unity, their solidarity.

Traditions teach and manifest values, and one's induction into traditions is at the same time an induction into the values of the group whose traditions they are. A group with shared traditions, accordingly, is a group with shared values. Human beings do not absorb values as abstractions, but as embedded in what they do.

This being so, not all traditions are *good.* Traditions are subject to reappraisal, renegotiation, and development. This can happen naturally and spontaneously, or in a self-conscious way, but if all the traditions of a group were permanently in dispute, they would lose their value as markers of identity, and the cultural group would be dissolved.

This is all to say that, if you see in the United Kingdom a high degree of concern with traditions connected with the political community, this is an indication of a state with a correspondingly high degree of solidarity. It is not *despite,* but *because* of, the power of the markers of identity belonging to the State, that the State can successfully incorporate into itself different cultural groups, without destroying either them or itself.

THE MONARCHY AS A CONSTITUTIONAL INSTITUTION

Political institutions are themselves traditions, under my definition. Unless they are brand new, they are passed to us from our

---

1 The phrase is "*captivi temporis præsentis*": Pope John Paul II, Apostolic Letter *Orientale Lumen* (1995), no. 8.

predecessors, and those under their authority characteristically feel they ought to continue the practices associated with them: elections, assemblies, and so on. If they are highly abstract, without ceremonial or culturally resonant appendages, it will be more difficult for them to serve as centres of solidarity.

Monarchies are particularly good at serving this function, because they are surrounded by traditions which serve as markers of identity and convey shared values. They cannot be created out of thin air; their historical rootedness is part of their value. But where they exist, they can perform the function of political institutions exceptionally well. For this reason, the many constitutional monarchies of the modern world, such as those of Japan, Thailand, and Belgium, serve as stabilising elements in their societies. States which have suffered a period of national trauma have restored their monarchies, such as Spain and Cambodia. And monarchies have proved resilient in times of constitutional crisis: obvious examples are Spain in the failed coup of 1981, the constitutional crisis in Australia in 1975, and, behind the scenes, in the UK in 1968.

The values embodied in the Christian symbolism of monarchy should have a special appeal to Catholics, for the same reason they have aroused the hostility of political radicals. The Christian monarchies of Europe found a model in the Old Testament, in which it is emphasised that the King is in a sense appointed by God, and rules as God's deputy: his "vicegerent."

This might sound like a recipe for arbitrary rule, but properly understood, it is the opposite. The kings of the Old Testament were subject to God's law and were held up to the mark by priests and prophets. A leader who claims to be the delegate of the people, on the other hand, can commit all kinds of crime in their name: whether because, as he claims, they desire it, or for their benefit. What prevents any constitutional leader from ruling tyrannically is a sense in which there is a higher law, something that limits his actions, that ensures both fair play in politics and justice to ordinary people. This obligation, ultimately, is to God, and is expressed more clearly by a head of state who is appointed by God, as it is generally expressed, than one appointed by "the people."

The religious symbolism of monarchy, therefore, should not be seen as the co-option of the Church to serve the State, but as the State's subordination to principles of justice which are ultimately interpreted by the Church. Stalin and the French revolutionaries were perfectly happy to co-opt the Church; what they did not want to do was to obey the Church.

It remains true that a wide range of constitutional arrangements are compatible with the Faith and have historically been blessed by the Church. The point is not that monarchy is the only legitimate form of government, just that it embodies in a uniquely clear way a Catholic understanding of political authority.

POMP AND CEREMONY

Some Catholics, upon whom a more puritanical aesthetic sense has rubbed off, see the pomp and ceremony of the British monarchy, on regular display in the State Opening of Parliament and with special outings for events like the Jubilee, royal funerals, and coronations, as something bad in itself: a waste of money, or the wrongful elevation of a mere human to an overexalted status. This is quite contrary to a traditional Catholic view, as expressed by an early chairman of the Latin Mass Society, Geoffrey Houghton-Brown, who deprecated the loss of the "canopy of state" in the ceremonial return of Cardinal John Heenan to Westminster Cathedral after being made a cardinal, in 1965. He wrote:

> I do not imagine that the Cardinal refused the customary canopy in order to be better seen [as suggested by the report in *The Times*] but in order to comply with the Pope's wish for 'simplicity'. If these customary symbols of high office are abandoned the office itself, be it of Pope, King, Bishop, Judge, or Mayor, will lose its significance, its dignity, its solemnity. By the sight of these symbols we recognise that which they represent. High Office must be made visible in order to be recognised and it can only be made visible by such symbolic and customary signs as the canopy of state, the crown, the mitre, the Judge's wig and robes, the Mayor's chain etc. Remove symbols and you lessen, even destroy, all respect, for authority.
>
> In connection with the canopy of state it should be noted that *The Times* (of February 26th) reported that 'The public Consistory has, however, lost some of its pomp, just as it has lost the great cardinal's hat[2] beneath which

---

2 That is, the scarlet galero, which continues to be seen above cardinals' coats of arms.

the new princes of the Church used to swear their oath
before the Pope—the great cardinal's hat has now vanished altogether from the formalities of creating members
of the Sacred College'.

In comparison with other reforms now taking place the
suppression of the cardinal's red hat may seem extremely
trivial but nonetheless it is extremely significant, indicating
as it does the loss of an emblem bound up with the history of the Roman Church. A generation that has no reverence for the past is doomed to become rootless, isolated,
adrift. This is the sin condemned in the commandment of
Moses,—if you do not hold your ancestors in honour you
will not keep for long the inheritance that they handed
down to you. The keeping of this commandment is the
secret of the miraculous survival of the Jewish race. It is
by the preservation of their ancient laws, festivals, fasts,
and liturgical language that the Jews have kept their racial
identity. Pope Paul is advocating a policy of ecclesiastical
suicide when he announces that the Church will despoil
herself—of that old royal mantle—in order to reclothe
herself in more simple manner suitable to the taste of
to-day. The disappearance of the canopy of state and
the red hat may be small matters but like certain small
marks on the body they can indicate a deadly disease.[3]

There is a parallel between eliciting respect for political and
ecclesiastical offices through the use of ceremonies, special apparel,
and symbolic objects, and the sacred liturgy: the Council of
Trent defended the pomp and ceremony found in the liturgy on
essentially the same lines.[4] Those of us who, like Houghton-Brown,
appreciate the important of dignity and solemnity in the liturgy,
can see the importance of pomp and ceremony in giving solemnity
to the office of the head of state, and those who attack it in one
context, tend to attack it in the other. Indeed, the monarchies
of Lutheran and Calvinist communities, in Scandinavia and the
Netherlands, have "despoiled" themselves of a good deal of the
symbolism of their office, and thus the significance of the office
along with it.

---

3 Geoffrey Houghton-Brown, *Notes on the Struggle to Retain the Roman
Liturgy, 1964–1972*, unpublished manuscript in the archives of the Latin
Mass Society, 1965, p. 3.
4 Council of Trent, Session 22, Chapter 5 (1562).

There is another aspect of pomp and ceremony which could usefully be mentioned. As Dr Francis Young has pointed out,[5] the key moments when one might have expected it to be trimmed—the accession of King James I in 1603 and the arrival of the Hanoverians in 1714—this was not done because the value of the traditional coronation ceremony in connecting the new kings to the English and British traditions of sacred monarchy was particularly important. King James wanted to be seen as a genuine monarch in France, since he inherited the claim to France that had been asserted by all English monarchs since Henry V. King George I needed the coronation service as a form of legitimation, given his weak claim on the throne. These examples underline the fact that the greater the complexity of the political community, and the greater the precariousness of the monarch, the more value there is in the symbolic affirmation of his leadership through impressive and mysterious ceremonies. These help bind together different national traditions, and ethnic and religious identities, as in the United Kingdom the Royal Coat of Arms combines heraldic elements from Britain's constituent nations, and the coronation throne incorporates the Stone of Scone, upon which the Scottish kings were once crowned.

THE BRITISH MONARCHY

None of this is to say that the British monarchy, or any of its recent incumbents, is perfect. Obviously, since 1558, with a brief respite from 1685 to 1688, our monarchs have been Protestant. Some were responsible for causing great suffering to Catholics. However, the experience of Cromwell's Commonwealth (1649–1660), in its treatment of Ireland, does not give us any grounds for thinking that other forms of government, such as a republic, would have been better. The problem was not that the British Isles were governed by hereditary monarchs, but that the State was for so long dominated by an intolerant Protestant elite. When this elite was confronted by a more Catholic-friendly monarch in the 1640s, and an actually Catholic monarch in the 1680s, it was the intolerant elite that triumphed, not the monarch. Indeed, King James II & VII was ousted by intolerant elite rebels precisely

---

5   "Holy Smoke" podcast with Damian Thompson, 5 May 2023.

because he had decreed religious liberty for all his subjects (including Jews and Muslims) in his two Declarations of Indulgence.

Queen Elizabeth II was a devout Protestant, preferring a fairly low-church style. The pageantry of the monarchy, supplemented for some members of the Royal Family by the ceremonial of Freemasonry, seems to have taken the place of what the original High Anglican, Archbishop Laud, called the "beauty of holiness."

To echo the Catholic martyr St Robert Southwell, when he was asked whether he wanted a Spanish invasion, I can say that I would like the Royal Family and the whole political elite to convert to Catholicism of their own free will. This is something for which Catholics in the United Kingdom pray and do penance. However, in the meantime, we must live with current realities.

First, it is clear, to all but a lunatic fringe, that Britain's new King, Charles III, is the legitimate head of state of our country. He deserves the loyalty of citizens like any head of state. Many French traditional Catholics join the French military because they believe in France, even if they aren't particularly keen on the Revolution which created the Republic. In the same way, British Catholics, even under persecution, have, by serving the Crown, wanted to give the lie to the accusation that their faith implied disloyalty. Should we pray for the King? Of course we should. At the traditional Catholic rite of the Mass, in England we have said special prayers for the monarch since the beginning of the long process of "Catholic emancipation" in 1778, prayers which are in other countries used for Catholic monarchs.[6]

Second, while the monarch and the Royal Family get drawn into politically fashionable causes, and while their role means that

---

6 The prayer, said in Latin, is translated as follows: "O Lord, save Charles our King, and mercifully hear us when we call upon Thee. Let us pray. We beseech Thee, almighty God, that Thy servant Charles our King, who through Thy mercy hast undertaken the government of this realm, may also receive an increase of all virtues. Fittingly adorned with these, may he be able to shun all evildoing [*in time of war:* to vanquish his enemies], and, together with the Queen consort and the royal family, being in Thy grace, to come unto Thee who art the Way, the Truth, and the Life. Through Christ our Lord. Amen." A translation of this (with variations for the previous monarch) was commanded to be said in churches after the Postcommunion Prayer at Mass on Trinity Sunday 2012, in the *Novus Ordo* rite of Mass, by the bishops of England and Wales, in honour of Queen Elizabeth II's Jubilee.

they studiously avoid party political partisanship, they remain an important cultural force. King Charles, for example, has lent his significant weight to combatting ugliness in architecture, and is patron of the Prayer Book Society, which defends traditional Anglican worship. He has often broadcast for the Catholic charity Aid to the Church in Need which aids and supports persecuted Christians worldwide. If the British monarchy disappeared it would be a calamitous setback for cultural conservatives of all kinds, with repercussions all over the globe.

Third, the ceremonial of the British monarchy has preserved its ancient Catholic character in a way that even the Catholic monarchies of Europe have not. The kings of Spain and Belgium, for example, do not even have coronation ceremonies. In many other ways, including simply by existing, the monarchy embodies and preserves our Catholic heritage. For example, the monarch personally gives alms to the poor on Maundy Thursday in a ceremony which preserves a Catholic tradition, abandoned in the Church's liturgy in 1955 when giving alms was removed from the *Mandatum*.

Can a Catholic be a republican? That is the wrong question. The default setting should be to support the existing constitution of one's country, if it is working reasonably well. The British monarchy has associations and resonances in Ireland which it does not have elsewhere, but even there the bitterness of the past is, increasingly, now in the past.

The Latin Mass Society of England and Wales organised a Requiem Mass for her late Majesty Queen Elizabeth, as the discipline of the Church allows, and a Mass of Thanksgiving for the Coronation. As Britons we honour our head of state; as Catholics we do that, in part, through the liturgy.

13
Honour a 'Heretic' King? The Question Facing King Charles III's Catholic Subjects

SEBASTIAN MORELLO

I T WASN'T LONG AFTER HER MAJESTY'S
death and the immediate ascent of King Charles III to
the throne, that some—far too many—Catholics started
yapping away on the internet about why they didn't like the
new king, how they disapproved of his chaotic family history, his
affiliation with globalists, his promotion of climate hysteria, and
his false religion. The US Catholic podcaster and vlogger, Taylor
Marshall, devoted a 51-minute-long video to explaining why King
Charles III is "an anti-Christ." (Incidentally, I was surprised to
discover that anyone still listened to Marshall, after his months
of going weak at the knees over the Trump presidency, during
which he repeatedly conflated the practice of Catholicism with
support for President Trump, whom he characterised as a new
Constantine providentially bestowed upon the world to bring in
a new Christian age. That didn't quite work out.)

Perhaps the first lesson to draw from the Common Doctor,
St Thomas Aquinas, is that one should not provide an explanation that is dependent on the supernatural where a natural
explanation is more appropriate: rather than saying that King
Charles is an "anti-Christ," we might say that he has at times
been a poor judge. In any case, after months of Marshall pre-
paring his followers to welcome the new Holy Roman Empire
under the reign of *Cæsar Donaldus*, it's fair to say that King
Charles is not the only one who is capable of poor judgment

(be careful Marshall, someone might call *you* an anti-Christ!).

For those Catholics of the United Kingdom and the Commonwealth who are wondering whether King Charles, head of State and Supreme Governor of the Church of England, with all his characteristics that they deem to be failings, is owed their loyalty and devotion, I give you the commandment of St Peter: "Love the brotherhood. Fear God. Honour the emperor" (1 Pet 2:17).[1]

Pope St Peter, chosen by Jesus Christ to be the visible leader of the Church, tells us that we must honour the emperor. Along with the imperatives to love the Church and fear God, we must honour our temporal lords. As an Englishman, King Charles is my sovereign, my head of state, and the parliamentary government that governs my country is *his* government—I must, then, honour him.

I remind my esteemed readers that St Peter, when he declared this commandment, was referring to Emperor Nero Claudius Cæsar Augustus Germanicus. Whatever the shortcomings of King Charles, they are nothing in comparison to those of Emperor Nero.

At the age of seventeen, Nero conspired with his mother to murder her husband, Nero's stepfather, the Emperor Claudius (by feeding him death-cap mushrooms). Claudius's son, the fourteen-year-old Britannicus, they then killed with a cup of poisoned wine. Nero's murderous mother, Agrippina, clearly imagined that she and her son would rule together, a suggestion from which Nero conveyed his dissent by attempting to drown her. The murder attempt failed, so Nero sent a slave to bludgeon his mother to death. Nero married two women, and then murdered both of them. He then took a mistress, Poppæa, with whom he had a child; but following an argument with Poppæa, he kicked her to death (when she was pregnant with his second child). Later, on noticing that one of his male slaves looked remarkably like his murdered mistress—whom he'd grown to miss—Nero had the unhappy slave castrated and then "married" him in what is history's first and only premodern same-sex marriage. Finally, Nero

---

1   The Greek word used here, as always when referring to the emperor, is βασιλεύς (Basileus), which literally means "king." This phrase is thus "Honour the King" in the Vulgate (*"regem honorificate"*), the Authorised Version, the Douai Rheims, and in many other translations.

likely burned down his own capital city, Rome, and then blamed the fire on the Christians. He then instigated the rounding up and slaughtering of Christians, a persecution that eventually led to St Peter himself being crucified under the still reigning Emperor Nero. Amidst all this, St Peter commanded the Church to "honour the emperor." Since we are obliged, according to that hallowed text inspired by the Holy Ghost, to honour the Emperor Nero, I think we can comfortably honour King Charles III.

The fact is that the British monarchy is the world's last Christian sacral monarchy,[2] one of the few remaining glimpses of living tradition that we have left, enabling us to peer into the glorious, ancient world of Christian kingship. Everything about the British monarchy, and indeed the coronation ceremony itself—always organised by England's senior Catholic layman, the Earl Marshal, the Duke of Norfolk—owes its existence to the medieval world of Catholic civilisation. The British monarchy is a gift to the world, and its incumbent is always owed our loyalty and devotion.

It is noteworthy that St John Henry Newman took his *Biglietto Speech*—delivered at the reception of the cardinalatial honour—as his opportunity to defend the sacral nature of the British monarchy and the establishmentarian settlement of Church and State in England:

> It must be recollected that the religious sects, which sprang up in England three centuries ago, and which are so powerful now, have ever been fiercely opposed to the Union of Church and State, and would advocate the un-Christianising of the monarchy and all that belongs to it, under the notion that such a catastrophe would make Christianity much more pure and much more powerful.

Newman was a true Tory. I don't mean a supporter of the modern UK Conservative Party, which is little more than a cabal of hyper-progressivist neo-Whigs. I mean Newman was a believer in the philosophy of *Toryism*: hierarchy, received culture and custom, corporatism, organicism, subsidiarity, and above all the consecration of

---

2 "Sacral," as sometimes used in a technical sense, refers to the transformation by grace of natural or "temporal" institutions, by which it is assumed into the life of the New Covenant. In this sense it can be contrasted with "sacred," which refers to those things that are of supernatural origin.

the realm by religious establishment. "Toryism . . . springs immortal in the human breast," Newman wrote to the Duke of Norfolk in 1875. For Newman, the great enemy England faced was the religious sects, the dissenters, who sought the separation of Church and State, thereby seeking to undermine the entire organic constitution of these Isles. Such sects, he claimed, wanted to secularise—perhaps overthrow, as they had succeeded in doing under Oliver Cromwell and his Puritan "roundheads"—the monarchy, and de-Christianise the nation. This, Newman asserted, would be a "catastrophe."

Newman, then, identified attacking the British monarchy and the Realm's establishmentarian Constitution with Protestant, dissenter sectarianism. And it follows from his view that Catholics yapping against the monarchy and the Constitution (of which the monarchy is a part), in effect reduce the Catholic Church to little more than just another sect within these Isles. But that is not what the Catholic Church *is*, nor what Newman understood her to be—rather, her claim is that of being the home of all the baptised. Catholics of the United Kingdom and the Commonwealth, by adopting such a reprehensible attitude rather than demonstrating their unswerving loyalty and devotion to their new liege lord, clearly have no understanding of the damage they are doing to the Church and her mission.

Nonetheless the Anglican Church is not the Church, I hear you exclaim, *but it is precisely another sect!* That may be true, but the fact is that most States today constitutionally declare that there is no true religion, or at least omit the possibility of identifying the true religion. In turn, it is assumed that the State is under no obligation to identify the true religion and enshrine that religion in its constitution. This is an error—namely, secularism—that the Catholic Church condemns (though her leaders are awfully quiet about it these days). England, however, constitutionally claims that there is a true religion and that the monarch is bound to defend it. It is of course unfortunate, from a Catholic perspective, that the State in this case has misidentified the true religion. Misidentifying the true religion, however, is absolutely preferable to denying—directly or indirectly—that there is such a *thing* as true religion.

But what about, I hear you ask, *the fact that King Charles III is a heretic?* Well, Nero wasn't even baptised, given he was a pagan. It is not, in any case, so clear that King Charles is a heretic. Of course, any member of the baptised who is not in full communion with Rome and holds beliefs that are contrary to the Catholic religion is *heretical*, but that is insufficient to say that such a person is *a heretic*, which entails formal commitment to heresy. One cannot be said to be a formal heretic unless that person has had his religious errors revealed to him, and it is known that this is so, and he has obstinately denied the truths that his erroneous religious commitments would require him to deny, and it is known that this is so. Without such qualifications, one cannot be said to be a formal heretic—when it comes to being a heretic, intention is key.

King Charles has met with popes, bishops, and plenty of lay Catholics; have any of them called him to the Catholic Faith? We have no idea. Nor do we know if, on having both the religious truth and his errors revealed to him, he obstinately rejected what he heard. Thus, we cannot say that he is *a heretic.*

There are inordinately excitable Catholics out there who believe that only a Catholic sovereign is owed their loyalty and devotion. When James Francis Edward Stuart—King James III of England and Ireland and James VIII of Scotland according to the popes and the Jacobite loyalists—died in 1766, Pope Clement XIII did not recognise the claim of James's son, "the Bonnie Prince," Charles Edward Stuart. Instead, the pope recognised the legitimacy of King George III, a Protestant claimant over a Catholic prince, and the pope fully expected King George's Catholic subjects to honour their king with their loyalty and devotion. Such a decision by a pope is hard to stomach for Jacobite sympathisers (like myself), but in hindsight it clearly belonged to the providential scheme of things: King George's United Kingdom was to become the foremost safe haven for Catholic emigres, both lay and clerical, fleeing the violence of the Terror following the French Revolution.

Perhaps modern Catholics increasingly prefer republicanism. They would do well to remember that the short history of modern, secular republics has not been a happy one, either for them or for the Church. Invariably, such republics were founded on the persecution of the Church's clerical leaders, consecrated religious, and temporal lords.

The Irish example is educational. The treasonous cause for an Irish republic was always a predominantly Protestant cause, from Wolfe Tone[3] onwards. For centuries, any Catholics who joined the rebels against their monarch were *de facto* excommunicated according to both the popes and the Catholic bishops of Ireland. Nonetheless, Irish rebels eventually got their way and created their explicitly anti-Catholic and aggressively secular constitution, symbolised by the tricolour flag that Ireland continues to fly. This constitution wasn't replaced with a more Christian-friendly constitution until 1937 at the instigation of Éamon de Valera, largely under the inspiration of the Jesuit political thinker Fr Edward Cahill. By that time, however, the damage had already been done, and now just look at Ireland, less than a century later.

Had Irish Catholics resisted being duped by their rebellious Protestant countrymen, and had, instead, remained loyal to their monarch and obeyed their bishops, over the years of growing Catholic emancipation, Catholicism would have likely risen to become a far more effective moral force in Ireland than it ever has been under the Republic. Instead, many Catholics sided with revolution, and they got their reward: an aggressively secular Ireland that seemingly hates the Catholic religion.

Catholics should learn a lesson from what happened to the Church in Ireland and respond by heeding the counsel of St Peter. They should honour their liege lord. King Charles, for all his shortcomings, is a dutiful man. His climate panics and enthusiasm for the "Great Reset" make me as uncomfortable as any reasonably sound person. But I have never expected my king to be correct on everything, just to uphold the settled constitution. As things stand, King Charles has shown every intention of doing just that. He has my loyalty and devotion, which are the minimum that should be expected of one of his subjects, Catholic or otherwise.

---

3   Irish revolutionary, lived 1763–1798.

14
Rex Sacrorum:
The Monarch as
a Sacred Symbol

Joseph Shaw

Introduction

ELSEWHERE IN THIS COLLECTION THE Coronation ceremonies of the British monarchy are discussed, remarkable survivals of the nation's Catholic past. These represent a culturally specific expression of something deeper and more universal: the monarch's role, in many cultures, in the sacred order. I express this in a deliberately vague way because this idea is not just found in Christian societies, but is applicable to the monarchies of pre-Christian Europe, to the Aztec monarchy, to the monarchies of the Far East, and indeed to monarchies in all kinds of religious and cultural settings. Importantly, it is also found in constitutional systems in which the monarch has little or no executive power, as well as in those in which he has a great deal. The Japanese monarchy before the Meiji Restoration would be an example of the former; even more striking, however, is what the Romans called the *rex sacrorum* (literally, "king of sacred things"), an office found not only in republican Rome but also in democratic Athens. Indeed, since we know quite a lot about the constitutions of these two states, and almost nothing about nearly all others of the ancient Greco-Roman world, there is no telling how widespread this office was. This was a person deputed to exercise the sacred duties of a king who otherwise has no constitutional existence. The monarch's sacred role was considered so important that a way had to be found for it to be exercised on behalf of the State, even when for all other purposes the monarchy had been abolished.[1]

The idea of a *rex sacrorum*, a role more typically combined with a monarch who has other constitutional and social roles, but surviving even without them, is helpful for the current debate about the monarchy particularly with a view to two oft-heard arguments. One is the argument that a non-executive monarch is a pointless appendage to what the influential British constitutional writer Walter Bagehot called the "efficient" (as opposed to the "dignified") part of the Constitution. That very distinction is sometimes taken to imply, contrary to what Bagehot intended, a rationalist rejection not only of the supernatural efficacy of religion, but of the power of symbols even at a natural level (see chapter 5).

The other argument is that the honour given to a monarch, particularly in a religious context, should be given only to God: that somehow a monarch gets in the way, between the individual, or society, and God.

The first argument, that a non-executive head of state is pointless, receives a practical answer from the widespread reality of non-executive heads of state worldwide today. Some of these have important reserve powers; some do not. Of those who have them, many never use them. And yet political scientists, constitution-writers, and ordinary citizens regard these figures as significant: most obviously, as separating the idea of the State from the idea of an elected government. Indeed, the separation of roles between head of state and head of government often adds stability to a constitutional settlement. However, important though that is, in this chapter I want to focus on the monarch's religious rather than political symbolism.

The second argument, that to elevate an individual as king is incompatible with giving proper respect to God, could also be answered in a practical way. Monarchies are today almost

---

1 See Livy, *History of Rome*, Bk. II, 2. Aristotle, or one of his collaborators, writing in the early Hellenistic period, notes that in the distant past, in Athens "the King occupied the building now known as the Bucolium, near the Prytanæum, as may be seen from the fact that even to the present day the marriage of the King's wife to Dionysius and its consummation take place there" (*Constitution of Athens* 3, trans. F. G. Kenyon, in *The Complete Works of Aristotle*, ed. Jonathan Barnes). This ceremony is otherwise mysterious.

invariably constitutional monarchies, so the existence of a monarch implies the separation of the role of head of state from that of head of government. If a monarchy ceases to exist, the question arises as to whether to adopt an executive head of state, or a non-executive one. The former kind of constitution is well-represented among nations today, and they raise the question: does not the elevation of a single man to both roles simultaneously imply a far more elevated level of worldly glory, if we are to speak in these terms, than having a head of state who is not also head of government? The pomp and ceremony associated with the presidencies of the United States of America and of the Republic of France is certainly far greater than that of most contemporary hereditary monarchs. The problem is generally mitigated somewhat, in practice, by time-limits on terms of office, but the handover of power between successive executive heads of state can be particularly fraught moments for less politically stable countries: and as recent events indicate, can be so even for such a paradigmatic democracy as the United States.

Again, however, I wish to leave aside the practical political implications of monarchy, in this chapter, to focus on the fundamental philosophical and spiritual issues. The argument that the office of king was somehow incompatible with giving honour to God was historically developed by the nonconformist Protestants who turned against the monarchy in the context of the seventeenth-century English Civil War. It is curious indeed to find it being used by Catholics some centuries after the ignominious collapse of the political project which it fuelled, Cromwell's Commonwealth. Its form, however, gives it a perennial appeal, as I hope to explain.

This paper is not an anthropological or historical study, although it will make reference to historical ideas and examples. It is an attempt to give a philosophical account of the sacred nature of monarchy, and the importance of this idea for a well-functioning society.

1. THE MONARCH AS A SACRED SYMBOL

Three cases from the ancient world

I wish to start the discussion by building up a sense of what I am talking about using examples. I choose three examples fairly well known in modern Western discourse, which can be said with confidence to have had no influence upon each other: Livy's description of the more-or-less mythical King Numa of Rome; Confucius's description of the mythical Chinese Emperor Shun, and other remarks of his; and the treatment of the kings found in the Hebrew Scriptures, the Old Testament. The classical Christian understanding of sacred monarchy is based on the third of these, though many Christian writers have also been familiar with Livy.

In ancient societies one of the key roles of the monarch was to offer sacrifice to the gods on behalf of the people, with a view to maintaining what the Romans called the *pax deorum:* a state of peace with the gods. However, this was not simply a matter of providing supernatural beings with large numbers of sacrificial victims: it included keeping oaths sworn with reference to the gods, and a general uprightness of life. Livy tells us that the second of Rome's kings, Numa, brought peace to Rome by instituting religious reforms (new temples, orders of priests, festivals, and so on), which brought about a general elevation of Rome's moral tone. Livy writes of the Romans after Numa's reforms:

> They became so much absorbed in the cultivation of religion and so deeply imbued with the sense of their religious duties, that the sanctity of an oath had more power to control their lives than the fear of punishment for law-breaking. Men of all classes took Numa as their unique example and modelled themselves upon him, until the effect of this change of heart was felt even beyond the borders of Roman territory. Once Rome's neighbours had considered her not so much as a city as an armed camp in their midst threatening the general peace; now they came to revere her so profoundly as a community dedicated wholly to worship, that the mere thought of offering her violence seemed to them like sacrilege.[2]

Livy's treatment of Rome's kings presents readers with a series of models, both good and bad, and Numa is the model of true religiosity. Livy's interest in religion is, however, tempered by the scepticism, often found in ancient writers, about some of the

---

2 Livy, *History of Rome*, Bk. I, 21, in *The Early History of Rome*, trans. Aubrey Sélincourt (London: Folio Society, 2006).

supernatural material he found in earlier sources. In this passage he focuses attention on religion's psychological effect on the population, whereas most ordinary Romans, and other pagans through the ages, would have seen the success of a programme like Numa's more directly in terms of divine favour: Rome had peace because the gods granted it to them as a result of Numa's actions. The two explanations are not mutually exclusive, of course. In any case, the role of the king is central.

The role of the monarch in maintaining the right ordering of society in a moral and spiritual sense can also find a place in a religious system which is not, or not very strongly, theistic, such as that of Confucius, and indeed, in his thought, this role of the Chinese emperors is brought very much to the fore.[3] For Confucius, the emperors' proper execution of "the rites" (in Chinese, *li*), a concept encompassing religious ceremonial (including the sacrificial cult) and a proper moral ordering of the whole of one's life, is key to the state of *ren*, generally translated "benevolence" or "humaneness" and the like. The connection between ritual correctness and ruling is implied by the phrase Confucius uses, "facing south," referring to the ritually correct stance of the emperor in his court, which can also be translated simply as "ruling." The ideal rule of the Emperor Shun, Confucius tells us, was simply to "fold his hands respectfully and face south."[4] The emperor's purity of heart, and piety toward ancestors and other spirits, brings about the peace of the empire (or the world: the word used means both). In short, if the emperor has virtue, the people will become virtuous.

As with the Roman example, some of Confucius's expressions could be understood to imply that the emperor brings this about by example: that is to say, by a natural, psychological effect on the people. However, there does seem to be something else as well: a mystical, spiritual power activated by the emperor's perfect conformity with *li*, flowing out over the whole empire. A truly upright man, Confucius taught, would pacify even the barbarians beyond the borders of China, were he to live among them.[5]

---

3 Confucius, *Analects*, trans D. C. Lau (London: Penguin, 1979), XII 1, IX 14, XII 17–18, XIII 1–2.
4 *Analects* XV 4.
5 *Analects* XV 6.

The role of personal deities in rewarding the just and punishing the wicked is not explicitly invoked by Confucius, and in
the classical Chinese context one could take his thinking in the
direction of Buddhism or Taoism to remove such beings still more
from the picture. In that case, it would simply be a matter of
the emperor's conformity to what is right which has the required
effect. Among the Romans, the Stoics could have read Numa's
success in a similar way, in terms of a perfect conformity to the
universal law of nature, a fact of such profound significance that
it stimulates a benevolent response from the very cosmos.

The role of the ruler is paralleled by the role of the head of a
household, the *paterfamilias*, and by anyone exercising authority
over a community. This would include temporary communities
like an army, or those on board a ship. As just noted, Confucius
imagines the mere physical presence of a true "gentleman" (as his
term for the upright man is sometimes translated) in the midst of
a community as having a salutary effect. The ruler of a city or
nation nevertheless has particular importance, with implications
for everyone within it.

The role of political leader and priest were often combined
in ancient societies. Even when a specialised class of priests was
well-established, the monarch would still often conduct sacrifices
in person on behalf of the community. Private persons would
do so in the context of their own domestic cults, on behalf of
themselves and their households, military commanders for their
armies, sea captains for their crews and passengers, and so on.

By contrast, in the course of the history of the kings of Judah,
my third example, the role of offering sacrifice became the exclusive prerogative of the hereditary priestly class, and it might be
imagined that this would lessen the importance of the king as
a sacred symbol. This, however, is not at all what happened.
Throughout the period of the monarchy, it is the king upon
whose fidelity to God the peace and prosperity of the people
depended. While there is a king, there seems to be no question
of attributing the good or bad fortunes of the kingdom to the
worthiness or unworthiness of the High Priest.

This is no less true of the narrative offered by the Bible's more
Temple-focused Books of Chronicles (or Paralipomenon) than it
is of the Books of Samuel and Kings, nor is it a matter simply of

the king's direction of religious policy, in relation to which there was a constant danger of giving way to religious syncretism or outright idolatry. Bad things are also threatened, or actually came about, for the whole community, from acts of injustice, like King David's extrajudicial murder of Uriah the Hittite (2 Sam 12); from symbolic encroachments on God's prerogatives, like David's calling of a census (2 Sam 24); and even from policies which imply a lack of trust in God, such as King Asa of Judah dealing with a military threat from the northern kingdom of Israel by bribing the King of Damascus to attack them (2 Chr 16:7–10). Kingly misdeeds might be public, or, like David's disposal of Uriah, a secret which a prophet would have to bring to light by divine inspiration.

The High Priest is of less significance precisely because it is not his role to govern the people in temporal matters. It was the king who led the people in war, determined taxes, and concluded treaties, and it was the success or failure of these tasks, alongside harvests and plagues, which manifested God's favour or disfavour. Thus, military disaster, famine, and plague were taken to imply a moral or spiritual failure of the king, and it was the king's repentance and penance which were critical in responding to it. This repentance and penance might be encouraged by the High Priest and by prophets, but it was the king above all who needed to undertake it, either alone, or leading the people in a collective act.[6]

Christian sacred monarchy

The example of the Old Testament was very important for the Christianised Roman imperial system, and for the Christian monarchies that emerged from the collapse of the original Western Empire, but in fundamental respects its influence was also in harmony with the attitude found among the pagan Romans, and indeed among the Celtic and Germanic peoples of late antiquity: all these would take it for granted that a tribal or national leader had a critical role in managing the relationship between the community and the spiritual realm. He would be guided in performing this role by specialised religious personnel, but they could not do it for him. The baptism of Clovis, King

---

6   See for example, 2 Samuel 12:16 and Jonah 3:6–10.

of the Franks, in 508, of Ethelbert, King of Kent, in 597, and of Grand Prince Vladimir of Rus in 988, could therefore be understood very naturally, by Christian observers and also by the kings' hitherto pagan subjects, as the baptism of the nation. Indeed, this is how the last of these events is often remembered: as the "baptism of Rus."

The subsequent history of Christian Europe, from the point of view of constitutional arrangements, is one of great complexity. The Church worked with all kinds of constitutional systems, and we find at different times various forms of republican, democratic (or more accurately, oligarchic) city states, and monarchies with a greater or lesser connection with a particular family, and therefore with a greater or lesser opportunity for choice among candidates on the part of some group of electors. There were also regions under the secular rule not only of the pope, but of "prince bishops," and even of religious orders (e.g., the Order of Malta and the Teutonic Knights). This bewildering variety of arrangements was possible only because the individuals at the apex of these states were able to perform the functions necessary for the stability and prosperity of the communities they governed. Among these functions was that of publicly representing the community in its dealings with matters divine.

It might be objected that in the context of Christianity, this was surely a role fulfilled by bishops and the pope. The foundation of the Catholic Church by Christ gave it a source of authority distinct from that of the civil ruler, and in crucial respects superior to it. Thus, St Thomas Aquinas, having noted the importance to the community of various skills (those of a doctor, tradesman, and teacher), remarks in *De Regno*:

> Now if man were not ordained to another end outside himself, the above-mentioned cares would be sufficient for him. But as long as man's mortal life endures there is an extrinsic good for him, namely, final beatitude which is looked for after death in the enjoyment of God, for as the Apostle says (2 Cor 5:6): "As long as we are in the body we are far from the Lord." Consequently, the Christian man, for whom that beatitude has been purchased by the blood of Christ, and who, in order to attain it, has received the earnest of the Holy Spirit, needs another and spiritual care to direct him to the harbour of eternal

salvation, and this care is provided for the faithful by the ministers of the church of Christ.[7]...

Thus, in order that spiritual things might be distinguished from earthly things, the ministry of this [spiritual] kingdom has been entrusted not to earthly kings but to priests, and most of all to the chief priest, the successor of St Peter, the Vicar of Christ, the Roman Pontiff.[8]...

Just as the king ought to be subject to the divine government administered by the office of priesthood, so he ought to preside over all human offices, and regulate them by the rule of his government.[9]

Thus, the king, taught the law of God, should have for his principal concern the means by which the multitude subject to him may live well. This concern is threefold: first of all, to establish a virtuous life in the multitude subject to him; second, to preserve it once established; and third, having preserved it, to promote its greater perfection.[10]

It is tempting for readers today to view these passages and others through the lens of modern conceptions of the separation of Church and State, but this would be a mistake.

First, although there is a specialisation of roles with regard to Church and State, Aquinas is not suggesting that spiritual matters are of no concern to temporal rulers. Rather, the king should be concerned above all else for the supernatural destiny of his subjects, but in acting on this concern he must call not only upon temporal knowledge and expertise, but supernatural knowledge and expertise, which the Church has taught him and concerning which the Church exercises ultimate authority. When it comes to this important aspect of human government, the king is a spiritual subject of the Church, just as prelates are his subjects in temporal matters.

Second, the other aspects of government, in which temporal authority acts within its own proper sphere, cannot be separated

---

7 Thomas Aquinas, *De Regno*, no. 105. From *On Kingship: To the King of Cyprus*, trans. Gerald B. Phelan (Toronto: Pontifical Institute of Mediæval Studies, 1982).
8 *De Regno*, no. 110.
9 *De Regno*, no. 114.
10 *De Regno*, nos. 116–17.

from morality or the cultivation of virtue. A major part of what temporal authority deals with is the execution of justice; then again, the virtue of subjects is critical to the peace of the State. Even from the perspective of "earthly things," the king has to see to the preservation of justice and the fostering of virtue.

Third, it must be kept in mind that while the Church was founded by Christ, the authority over temporal things exercised by temporal rulers also derives from God and is exercised under divine authority. The notion of the king as a *vicegerent*, a deputy, of God, elevates the dignity of earthly power and also subordinates it firmly to the Law of God: though not to holders of spiritual authority. As Pope Pius XI expressed it much later:

> Our Lord's regal office invests the human authority of princes and rulers with a religious significance; it ennobles the citizen's duty of obedience. It is for this reason that St Paul, while bidding wives revere Christ in their husbands, and servants respect Christ in their masters, warns them to give obedience to them not as men, but as the vicegerents of Christ; for it is not meet that men redeemed by Christ should serve their fellow-men. "You are bought with a price; be not made the bond-slaves of men" [1 Cor 7:23]. If princes and magistrates duly elected are filled with the persuasion that they rule, not by their own right, but by the mandate and in the place of the Divine King, they will exercise their authority piously and wisely, and they will make laws and administer them, having in view the common good and also the human dignity of their subjects.[11]

I remarked on the Davidic monarchy that, although the sacrificial cult became the exclusive preserve of the Temple priesthood, the king remained the focus of the question of good government: whether God would be pleased, or angered, by the community's conduct of its affairs. To a large extent this remains true for Christian monarchy. The Church possesses ultimate authority (under God) over spiritual things, but in important respects the practical exercise of this authority depends on the cooperation of the king who, furthermore, even in exercising his temporal authority, must do so in the interests of justice and virtue and with the fearful

---

11   Pope Pius XI, Encyclical *Quas Primas*, no. 19.

consciousness that he is exercising God's authority. Just as with the Old Testament's good King Josiah and bad King Manasseh, the divine favour or disfavour towards a community as a whole is crucially the responsibility of the king, a responsibility which churchmen can, for the most part, only exhort him to fulfil.

As noted above, the variety of constitutional arrangements found in the Middle Ages, and since, is not incompatible with this picture, since there will still be someone at the apex of the state who can do what a king is supposed to do. However, while this is true in relation to a king's executive functions, when it comes to his *symbolic* role, monarchy has important advantages, as I will explain next.

The symbolism of the sacred monarchy

It is interesting to note that of Aquinas's arguments, for the advantages of a monarchy over alternative forms of government in *De Regno*, some are of a practical nature—as when he says that having a single ruler avoids intractable disagreements—but others are of a symbolic nature.

> Wherefore also in all things that are ordained towards one end, one thing is found to rule the rest. Thus, in the corporeal universe, by the first body, i.e., the celestial body, the other bodies are regulated according to the order of Divine Providence; and all bodies are ruled by a rational creature. So too in the individual man, the soul rules the body; and among the parts of the soul, the irascible and the concupiscible parts are ruled by reason. Likewise, among the members of a body, one, such as the heart or the head, is the principal and moves all the others. Therefore, in every multitude there must be some governing power.[12]

Aquinas sees the role of the king as parallel not only to that of God, but to a whole set of things arranged hierarchically above and below him.

The first parallel involves the celestial bodies: that is, the stars and planets. In the Aristotelian-Ptolemaic understanding of the universe, found very fully described by Dante and not too dissimilar to Plato's cosmology, the earth is the centre-point

---

12 *De Regno*, no. 9.

of the orbits of the celestial bodies, which were thought of as being at different, but fixed, distances from the earth. Thus, each orbit could be described as a "sphere" enclosing the earth. The outermost sphere, that of the stars, was understood to determine the course of the one within it, and so on through the successive spheres, and these were also understood to be the causes of movement of living things on the earth itself. The causation in question is simultaneous, efficient causation, like a ball being moved by a stick in continuous contact with it, and the stick being moved by the hand holding it. Contrary to that example, however, this does not exclude the exercise of free will when it comes to human actions, as I will explain. The planets themselves were understood as, or as being moved by, living, intelligent, and imperishable beings.

For present purposes, the point of Aquinas's analogy can be described in this way. The chief celestial body (the starry sphere) governs the inner spheres and the earth itself through the harmonious mediation of the hierarchy of the other spheres. By analogy, the king governs his subjects through the (ideally) harmonious hierarchy of lords and tenants, or of his officers.

Movement at the lower levels involves free choice for rational agents, in this sense. The higher level gives the end towards which the lower level moves, but the lower has choice over the means to be taken to the end. One the one hand, our objective is fixed: for humans, it is "happiness." The debate about the means to this end can merge, however, with a debate about what happiness *is:* wealth, power, pleasure, or virtue. Similarly, in Aristotle's example, the goal of the bridlemaker is fixed by the rider, who needs the bridle for a particular purpose; the goal of the rider is fixed by the military commander, the commander by the statesman. All exercise autonomy in their tasks but are subject to the judgement of their superior, as to whether they have succeeded or not.

All activity would instantly come to a halt if the topmost agent in the series ceased to give its impetus, like the hand guiding the stick and the stick the stone. Furthermore, the creature at the top of the hierarchy must be intelligent: it doesn't simply follow the goal, but understands it, and it is this goal that it directs those beneath it to follow. The end is given to it by the Creator, God, who is the ultimate apex of the hierarchy.

In the case of the king, the goal of action is the common good. This goal is not chosen by the king but is implicit in the nature of kingship; as just explained, choice entails the question of how to pursue it, and what it means.

As well as presenting us with a pleasing image of the parallel hierarchies, Aquinas wished with his analogy to emphasise the fact that the apex must be single, rather than a system of two or more chief officers as was sometimes found in the ancient world: Rome had two consuls, for example, and Sparta two kings. Inevitably one of these was senior to the other, but these systems were nevertheless intended to prevent one person gaining too much power and prestige, by establishing a colleague with almost as much. What Aquinas is saying in the first passage is a message repeated elsewhere in *De Regno*, that it is in the nature of things for *movement* to have a single source, of which a hierarchy of authority is an example. Otherwise, there could be movements going in different directions, which would bring into question the unity of the subject: the political community.

Another, implicit, analogy is relevant here: that, in Aristotelian science, different characteristic activities or natural directions of movement are an essential part of the identity of different species, and just as humans are living things that pursue happiness by definition, so different kinds of humans pursue different conceptions of happiness. A political community, then, would be a kind of thing which by definition pursues the common good; different kinds of community could have different conceptions of this: say, communities with predominantly mercantile or agrarian interests. A community with irreconcilable conflicting interests is going to have trouble.

This is exactly what happens, in fact, when reason fails to rule the two non-rational parts of the soul, the irascible and concupiscible parts, and this is what Aquinas mentions next. When reason is not on its guard, a human agent can end up acting out of anger (arising from the irascible part of the soul) or appetite (from the concupiscible part), unguided by rational judgement, and typically the result will be bad actions. In this passage Aquinas focuses on the good case in which the reason is properly in charge, but the contrasting case inevitably comes to mind. Similarly, if a "multitude" lacks a single directing lead, then it would fall prey to confusion and conflict.

In this way, in this passage, the authority of a king parallels the governing role of the chief celestial body, under God, over the cosmos, on a vast scale, and of the rational soul in the body, on a smaller scale. In another passage, this latter parallel is expanded upon by Aquinas:

> Therefore let the king recognize that such is the office which he undertakes, namely, that he is to be in the kingdom what the soul is in the body, and what God is in the world. If he reflect seriously upon this, a zeal for justice will be enkindled in him when he contemplates that he has been appointed to this position in place of God, to exercise judgment in his kingdom; further, he will acquire the gentleness of clemency and mildness when he considers as his own members those individuals who are subject to his rule.[13]

Here, Aquinas tells us that the king is like the soul (or mind) in a body. On the one hand, the authority of the king is illustrated by comparison with the control exercised by the mind over the body; on the other, the benevolence one feels for one's own body is the model for what the king should feel about his subjects.

There is, however, more to it than this, because to a Christian reader this second idea will evoke a well-known metaphor used by St. Paul to illustrate the authority of a husband over his wife and of Christ over his Church: that of head and body.

> The husband is the head of the wife, as Christ is the Head of the Church. He is the saviour of his body. Therefore, as the Church is subject to Christ, so also let wives be to their husbands in all things.... So, also, ought men to love their wives as their own bodies. He that loveth his wife, loveth himself. For no man ever hated his own flesh; but nourisheth and cherisheth it, as also Christ doth the Church: Because we are members of His body, of His flesh, and of His bones.[14]

So once again, the king in his kingdom is placed into the context of parallels at both a larger scale—of Christ and the Church— and at a smaller scale—of a husband and wife.

It is striking that despite the constitutional variety of his own

---

13   *De Regno*, no. 94.
14   Ephesians 5:23–24, 28–30.

day, Aquinas expresses such a decided preference for monarchy. He does so not only for practical reasons—the brisk efficiency of a thirteenth-century executive monarch, with his networks of personal and family loyalties—but also for symbolic reasons deeply embedded in the Catholic worldview. The king slots into an interlocking series of ruler-ruled relationships, with God's rule over the cosmos at one end, and the individual rational soul's rule over the body at the other, with Christ and the Church, and the husband and his family, in between.

In these cases, it is not executive power which is primarily at issue, but the symbolic connection between one level of rule and the next. The different spheres of the heavenly bodies, the husband, the rational soul, and the king, each represents the submission of the subordinate level to the superior level, and ultimately to God. It is no matter that what we may be tempted to regard as the "real work"—the executive functions—of a king may be performed by his ministers, any more than it matters that the influence of the starry sphere is mediated through the other spheres before it reaches the earth. What is symbolically crucial is that at each level rule is represented by a *single* entity—the celestial body, the husband, the mind, or the monarch—because it represents to its immediate subordinates the single God who crowns the whole cosmic hierarchy.

Given this symbolic role for the head of state, it is obviously preferable to have one who is able to identify himself with the role to the greatest extent possible. A head of state who is elevated above party politics and brought up to the role as heir to a hereditary office is clearly preferable, from the point of view of sacred symbolism, to a constantly changing and politically divisive figure. The practical disadvantages in modern conditions of an executive hereditary monarch can, on the other hand, be avoided by making the office non-executive.

In trying to get clear about exactly what Aquinas meant in the rather dense passages I have quoted I have spent quite a lot of time on the cosmological worldview which he derived from Aristotle, and also Aristotle's theory of human action. Aquinas's essential insight, however, is not tied to the scientific validity of this model. It can be seen as a highly elaborated version of a very simple idea, one common to the other historical and cultural contexts discussed earlier: that the monarch is the key to a society's relationship with what we might call the spiritual realm. This is important to my argument because I need to show that even in a Christian context, even for Aquinas, this remains true, despite the role of the Church in spiritual affairs: for Aquinas, and other Catholic political theorists, the secular ruler is the means through which God's will is mediated to a community in relation to temporal affairs.

To repeat, the temporal/spiritual distinction is not a secular/ religious distinction in the modern sense. There is no non-religious sphere of life in premodern thought: the word "secular" in this context simply means "pertaining to the *sæculum,*" the current age, as opposed to eternity: which is to say, "temporal things," or "the world." The distinction is, rather, between those means and goals which relate to eternal things, and those which focus on temporal things. God's will is normative for each, and God is the only source of authority for either. If we want to know who mediates divine authority for a political community, considered as a political community, it is the secular ruler. The kind of ruler who symbolises this best is a single, lifelong ruler, wholly taken up in a role conceptualised as sacred: that is, a king.

2. The Monarch as Intermediary

Liberalism and radical Protestantism

In St John Henry Newman's famous *Biglietto Speech* (already quoted in the last chapter), which he delivered when he was made a cardinal in 1879, he remarked:

> It must be recollected that the religious sects, which sprang up in England three centuries ago, and which are so powerful now, have ever been fiercely opposed to the Union of Church and State, and would advocate the un-Christianising of the monarchy and all that belongs to it, under the notion that such a catastrophe would make Christianity much more pure and much more powerful.[15]

Newman's focus in the speech is what he calls "liberalism," which he defines as "religious indifferentism": in his words in the same speech, "Liberalism in religion is the doctrine that there is no positive truth in religion, but that one creed is as

---

15 St John Henry Newman, *Biglietto Speech*, 12 May 1879.

good as another." Religious liberals accordingly find intolerable the manifestation of any particular religious creed by the state, because this places one religion ahead of others. Newman connects liberalism in its British manifestation with the political reality of religious pluralism. As he explains:

> Every dozen men taken at random whom you meet in the streets has a share in political power—when you inquire into their forms of belief, perhaps they represent one or other of as many as seven religions; how can they possibly act together in municipal or in national matters, if each insists on the recognition of his own religious denomination?

The conceptual connection between religious liberalism and British Protestant nonconformity is less clear. The splintering of the religious landscape after the Reformation was a result of the State's failure to restrain Protestant dissent (as well as Catholicism), but that was not a result the dissenters themselves planned or desired. The earlier Protestants, at least, would have preferred everyone to agree with them, and thereafter to have used State power to preserve the purity of religion, as happened in Calvin's Geneva and the Puritan communities of the American colonies. But as their thinking developed, many of them found themselves opposed to the institution of the monarchy, in the context of the execution of King Charles I in 1649, and came to reject the public manifestation of religion, including the religious symbolism that continued to be associated with the monarchy after the Restoration.[16]

I cannot, within the scope of this chapter, delve too deeply into the seething cauldron of theological debate among seventeenth-century Protestants, but this is explored a little more in chapter 3, where James Bogle discusses the Protestant use of the phrase *soli Deo gloria*, understood to mean "to God alone be glory." As Bogle explains, this phrase is a distortion of 1 Timothy 1:17: "*immortali invisibili soli Deo honor et gloria*," "honour and glory to the immortal, invisible *one* only God." Nevertheless, the phrase was used by Protestants to reject the giving of glory or veneration

---

16 Even so, Congregationalists, Independents, and some other Puritans nevertheless maintained an official State Church in their American colonies right up until 1833, when Massachusetts became the last state in the Union to separate Church and State.

to the saints and to human leaders alike, a radical spiritual and political egalitarianism and a total rejection of the hierarchical principle set out in the last section. The kind of Protestant who wanted to advance this slogan was, for example, often opposed to the office of bishop, but the principle did not stop there, leading King James VI and I to make his famous remark: "No bishop, no king."[17]

One anecdote will suffice to illustrate the theory. The historian of Protestantism, Alec Ryrie, recounts the story of a seventeenth-century Quaker serving girl, Elizabeth Andrews, who refused to curtsey to her employer, Lord Newport. "He teasingly offered her £20 if she would. She replied that even if he offered her his entire estate, 'I durst not do it, for all honour belongeth to God.'"[18] This idea is part of Protestantism's radical disintermediation: the stripping out of those persons or institutions which stand in some sense between God and the individual believer. The individual is to discern God's will directly, from the Bible, or from private inspiration, without the guidance of the Church as an authoritative interpreter, or a bishop or pope as enjoying teaching authority. The individual is to pray to God directly, without the mediation of the Blessed Virgin Mary, the saints, or the angels, or the public prayer of the Church. The individual is saved, if he is saved, directly, by God, without the need for the human institution of the Church or the sacramental system.

This is not incompatible with the use of a rite of baptism, for example, as long as this is understood only as a sign, not something either necessary for salvation or really efficacious (causing a genuine "regeneration," rebirth, a washing away of Original Sin). Then again, traditions of interpretation, theologically authoritative individuals, and institutional structures inevitably arose among radical Protestants, but these were always *ad hoc* and fragile, and this kind of Protestantism was always highly fissiparous, liable to split over doctrinal differences.

The ability of Protestants to accept all sorts of formal arrangements, including even bishops, on occasion, without believing in

---

17 Quoted in David Harris Wilson, *King James VI and I* (London: Jonathan Cape Press, 1956), 279.
18 Alec Ryrie, *Protestants: The Radicals Who Made the Modern World* (New York: HarperCollins, 2017), 128.

them in the traditional way, is a confusing aspect of the situation. A sixteenth-century "moderate Puritan" like Edmund Grindal, who rejected the sacrament of Holy Orders, could assume the title of archbishop of Canterbury as an administrative convenience, or perhaps as a decorative feature of Anglicanism that reassured religious conservatives, while not thinking there was anything intrinsically problematic about religious communities which did not have bishops: indeed, this has been the position of most of his successors down to the present day.

This contrasts very much with Aquinas's hierarchical vision of the world. The hierarchy of the celestial spheres, of the angelic choirs, of the Church, of the family, or of temporal rulers, is one in which each link in the chain is causally efficacious: it is a real, moving part, a link in the causal chain. As I noted, the scientific model of the day stressed simultaneous causation—the hand moving the stick, the stick moving the stone—and held it as an axiom that each link in the chain is necessary to the transmission of the causal impulse. We might prefer to think of a line of falling dominos, or a cable carrying an electrical current. In other kinds of hierarchy, a leapfrogging of intermediate steps may be possible and occasionally necessary—a Field Marshal can command a Private soldier, for example—but this does not make the other ranks redundant, and it is not in any sense *better* for the command to come directly from the top than for it to go through the intermediate ranks in the normal way.

Hierarchy and causation

The archaic scientific paradigm Aquinas worked with should not blind us to the significance of the contrast between his view and the radical Protestant one. Archbishop Grindal viewed the succession of bishops, as I just noted, as spiritually non-functional, with the real work being done directly between God and the individual. The scientific parallel would be to see, in the succession of falling dominos, one domino as not having any real causal power over the next domino, but each being toppled over directly by God. This view, called occasionalism, is the application to science of the principle of what I have called disintermediation: the only real causation is that of God, as opposed to what Aquinas called "secondary causation."

The adoption of Aristotelian science by Catholic thinkers in the thirteenth century was crucial for the later scientific revolution because, despite its flaws, it directed investigators' attention to the individuals at each point in the chain of causes. Unlike Platonism, which attributed causal efficacy to abstract entities in the Realm of Forms, Aristotle insisted that causal powers were to be found in the individual: as he said, "man begets man; universal Man does nothing." If you want to know how sea-turtles reproduce, Aristotle tells us, don't just engage in intellectual contemplation of the concept of "sea-turtle," like the Platonists; nor should you attribute everything directly to God, like the radical Protestants. You should go and examine some sea-turtles.

This scientific instinct was a good fit for Catholicism because, as Catholic theologians had been insisting for many centuries, the institutional Church, the sacraments, and the individual believer, are not just play-acting: they have real causal significance in the economy of salvation, something which is true alongside the reality that it is all, ultimately, radically dependent upon God. The parallel holds true in all the areas of life in which there are intermediaries between the individual and God.

Fallen nature and the purification of religion

Part of the motivation for Protestant disintermediation is to focus all attention upon God. Another part is to turn attention away from created things. In that Protestant view, God alone deserves glory, because, as Bogle notes, on this view the whole of creation is radically corrupted by sin. Catholics too believe that sin has affected the world in a profound way, but not in such a way that, for example, it is inappropriate to use art to praise God or reason to investigate Him. These created things can be purified, even redeemed. For the radical Protestant, this is impossible, so the purity of religion consists of removing created things from it, as much as possible.

This explains Newman's description of the Protestant sects as thinking that a de-Christianised monarchy would "make Christianity much more pure and much more powerful." They might concede that the monarchy, or something like it, is politically necessary, but they would much rather it had no place in the public manifestation of religion. In a similar way, they would rather fine music, or subtle intellectual endeavour, or complex hierarchy, if they must exist, had no place in evangelisation. It is inappropriate to place any of these things between the individual believer and the Almighty, because as created things they are affected by sin and associated with human pride.

Of course, created things cannot be entirely evicted from religious affairs, but this general tendency of thought leads to radical simplification, in music, art, and architecture, and to anti-intellectualism and radical egalitarianism. The Protestant hope, as Newman expressed it, was that a purified religion would be "much more powerful," because the extraneous elements are holding it back.

The force of this way of thinking is well expressed by the influential modern Lutheran theologian Karl Barth, who did not simply argue that philosophical arguments for the existence of God don't work, or don't produce genuine theological Faith, or tend to get in the way of a trusting acceptance of God's self-revelation. Rather, he argued that a philosophical argument for the existence of God, would, if accepted, lead the philosopher to believe not in God at all, but in a false god, an idol of his own making.[19] Human reason as an intermediary between the individual and God will actually *divert* the individual *away* from God, towards something else entirely, something positively evil.

The influence of radical Protestantism and the monarchy

The long transition from the world of the thirteenth century to the present was characterised by the rise of individualism. This may have been driven above all by economic and technological developments, but the process was defended and justified, and opposition to it brushed aside, by reference to an ideology, notably the claim that those things which impede individualism represent unreasonable restrictions on liberty and are an affront to the dignity of the individual. This ideology, as we experience it today, is the descendent of the claims of radical Protestants of (now) four or five centuries ago.

Similarly, while only a small remnant of hardline Protestants today still believe in the radical depravity of the created world, in aesthetic judgements the association of "purity" with "simplicity"

---

19 Karl Barth, *Church Dogmatics in Outline* (London: SCM Press, 1949).

is still culturally powerful. The cultural history of England, and of Anglicanism, has been characterised by a prolonged struggle between the tendency to simplify, cut down, individualise, and equalise, and attempts to retain or recover complexity, decoration, and hierarchy, often with reference either to the Catholic past, or Catholic influences from abroad.

The British monarchy is the outstanding example of something preserved from the Catholic past. It is not just that it stands, in politics and law, between the individual and the God from whom all power comes—any head of state will do this, on Christian principles—but that this mediation is not something to be played down, and be embarrassed about, but to celebrate, and venerate.

This institution is an affront to the radical Protestant instinct, which would say that if a leader is absolutely necessary, he should be distinguished as little as possible from everyone else, because he represents a danger of venerating something other than God, something that is created and therefore evil to venerate. On the contrary, the Catholic instinct is that the means by which, in the circumstances of our own history and traditions, God's authority is mediated to us, is worthy of veneration *precisely because* God is worthy of veneration.

The angels and saints, even our Blessed Lady herself, are nothing without the grace of God. Since God's grace has made them something, the Catholic principle says: let us recognise this fact by according them the respect which possessing this grace makes them deserve. The pope, the bishops, and the clergy in general are nothing without God's grace, and may not even be worthy individuals, but their office gives them genuine dignity because it was established by God to make possible our spiritual government and the provision of the sacraments. The king, too, whatever his personal qualities, warrants our respect because the office he holds is a glorious one: God has made it so, by giving him the position, in accordance with law and custom.

CONCLUSION

As noted in the first part of this chapter, the idea that the institution of the monarchy is a fitting symbol of the community's interface with the spiritual realm is not simply a Catholic one, but one which is common to a great variety of cultures and traditions.

It is Protestantism, and the individualism and egalitarianism it has spawned, which is the outlier.

A monarch, particularly in the British tradition, is not simply just another kind of head of state. To repeat what I noted earlier, because this is a sacred office, it is one with which the officeholder must as much as possible be identified, and a single, hereditary, lifelong appointment reflects the source of this authority better than any other.

The disappearance of the monarchy would represent the triumph of a secularised version of the Protestant revolt against the Catholic tradition, which itself reflects the common patrimony of all traditional societies. Whereas the radical Protestant wanted to remove the monarch to see God more clearly, his modern descendant has come to see the flattening and erasing of all hierarchy and complexity as an end in itself. The glory goes not to man, and not to God, but is simply expunged from the world.

The modern ideal is manifested all around us: architecture which eschews beauty, music too sophisticated for harmony, food lacking taste, relationships without commitment. The supposed utilitarian advantages of unencumbered and aerodynamic modern institutions are in practice overwhelmed by the loss of a sense of continuity, stability, familiarity, and connection with the spiritual, all things which make for a sense of social solidarity.

Solidarity, the sense of common interest with other members of the community, is perhaps the key concept that explains the connection between our political and cultural traditions, and matters of practical politics, such as family breakdown and what happens in a civic emergency: whether people rally round to help each other, or loot the nearest shops. A recognisable hierarchy in which a monarch connects the community with the divine, as a comprehensible symbolic system unifying the state, is of no small account in underpinning solidarity. Not to be neglected either, however, is the vocation this system gives to the monarch himself: to be a symbol, not only of national unity, but of the right ordering of things. As Confucius put it: "to fold his hands in a respectful fashion, and face south."

O Lord, save Charles our King, and mercifully hear us when we call upon thee.

Let us pray. We beseech thee, almighty God, that thy servant Charles our King, who through thy mercy hast undertaken the government of this realm, may also receive an increase of all virtues. Fittingly adorned with these, may he be able to shun all evildoing [*in time of war:* to vanquish his enemies], and, together with the Queen consort and the royal family, being in thy grace, to come unto thee who art the way, the truth, and the life. Through Christ our Lord. Amen.

Prayer at the conclusion of the principal
Mass on Sunday in England and Wales,
when celebrated according to the 1962 Missal.

ACKNOWLEDGEMENTS

Chapter 1, "The Monarchy and the British Constitution," by James Bogle and Sebastian Morello, was first published at the *OnePeterFive* website, 29 November 2022.

Chapter 3, "The Monarchy and Responsibility for Legislation," by James Bogle, was published in an earlier version at the *Rorate Cæli* website, 11 December 2022.

Chapter 5, "Lost Dignity: On the Dignified Aspect of Government and the Problem of Totalitarianism," by Sebastian Morello, will be published in a forthcoming issue of *The European Conservative.*

Chapter 6, "The Coronation is a Ritual Humiliation," by Sohrab Ahmari, was first published at the *UnHerd* website, 5 May 2023.

Chapter 7, "An Eighth Sacrament?," by Charles Coulombe, was first published at the *OnePeterFive* website, 14 March 2023.

Chapter 8, "The Vocation of Queen Elizabeth II and the Coronation Liturgy," by Peter Day-Milne, is a developed version of two articles published at *The European Conservative* website: "Queen Elizabeth and Christian Monarchy, Part I: The Servant-Queen" (17 October 2022) and "Queen Elizabeth and Christian Monarchy, Part II: Restoration of the Christian Ideal" (2 May 2023).

Chapter 11, "The Place of the Monarchy in Anglophone Culture," is based on an earlier version published as "The Place of the Monarchy in Anglican Culture," in Tracey Rowland, *The Anglican Patrimony in Catholic Communion: The Gift of the Ordinariates* (London: Bloomsbury, 2021).

Chapter 12, "On Monarchy and Tradition," by Joseph Shaw, was first published at the *OnePeterFive* website, 12 September 2022, under the title "Why British and Commonwealth Catholics Venerate Their Protestant Monarch."

Chapter 13, "Honour a 'Heretic' King? The Question Facing King Charles III's Catholic Subjects," by Sebastian Morello, was first published at *The European Conservative* website, 26 September 2022.

We are grateful for the permission to reprint these pieces. All other chapters appear here for the first time.

Contributors

Mr Sohrab Ahmari is a widely published writer, a founder and editor of *Compact* and a contributing editor at *The American Conservative*. His books include *The Unbroken Thread* (2021) and *Tyranny, Inc.* (2023), both published by Penguin Random House.

James Bogle Esq is a British barrister (trial attorney) educated at the Middle Temple and the Inns of Court School of Law, London, at the Royal Military Academy, Sandhurst, and at Melbourne University, and has been involved in a number of constitutional cases in the British courts such as *R (on the application of Miller and another) v Secretary of State for Exiting the European Union* [2017] UKSC 5. A former acting Head of his Chambers, he also practises in banking and commercial law and in public law, particularly in end-of-life cases. He is also an historian, writer, former British cavalry officer, and convert to the Catholic Faith, and writes for *The European Conservative, OnePeterFive, Rorate Cæli, The Catholic Herald,* and other publications. He is the co-author of a biography of the last Austrian Emperor, Charles I.

Mr Charles Coulombe is the author of many books, including *Blessed Charles of Austria: A Holy Emperor and His Legacy* (TAN, 2020), *A Catholic Quest for the Holy Grail* (TAN, 2017), and *Puritan's Empire: A Catholic Perspective on American History* (Tumblar House, 2008). His writings have appeared in *The Catholic Herald, Crisis,* and *The European Conservative;* he also has his own podcast with Mr Vincent Frankini, "Off the Menu."

Mr Peter Day-Milne read Classics at Trinity College, Oxford and then undertook further studies in philosophy and history. He has written for *The European Conservative, Adoremus,* and other publications.

Dr Sebastian Morello holds a BA in philosophy from the Open University and MA and PhD degrees in philosophy from the University of Buckingham. His postgraduate supervisor was Sir Roger Scruton. Morello is the author of *The World as God's Icon*

(Angelico Press, 2020), which explores the Neoplatonic themes present in the metaphysical realism of Thomas Aquinas, and *Conservatism and Grace* (Routledge, 2023), a work of political philosophy. He is also a contributing author of numerous books on philosophy, history, liturgy, and education. Presently, Morello works as Senior Editor, Editorial Board Member, and writer at *The European Conservative*, a journal of political and cultural criticism. He lives in Bedfordshire, England, with his wife and children.

DR JOSEPH SHAW'S studies at Oxford University culminated in a Doctorate in Philosophy, and he was a member of Oxford University's philosophy faculty for eighteen years. During that time, he taught moral philosophy, Aristotle, Aquinas, and the philosophy of religion, and published academic papers on philosophy of religion and ethics. He is Chairman of the Latin Mass Society of England and Wales and President of the International *Una Voce* Federation (FIUV). He is the editor of *The Case for Liturgical Restoration* (Angelico Press, 2018) and *The Latin Mass and the Intellectuals: Petitions to Save the Ancient Mass from 1966 to 2007* (Arouca Press, 2023), and the author of *The Liturgy, the Family, and the Crisis of Modernity* (Os Justi Press, 2023). He blogs at lmschairman.org.

INDEX OF NAMES